The first pre-series Class 800 IEP train under test at Network Rail's Rail Innovation and Development Centre. HITACHI

COVER PICTURE: 60163 *Tornado* prepares to set out into the night from Wansford station with its demonstration freight on January 4, 2019.
MARTIN VOS

COVER INSETS: *Locomotion* on display at the Head of Steam museum.
DARLINGTON BOROUGH COUNCIL

The Hitachi plant at Newton Aycliffe.
HITACHI

AUTHOR:
Jonathan Webb

PRODUCTION EDITOR:
Pauline Hawkins

DESIGN:
Craig Lamb
Kriele Ltd
design_lamb@btinternet.com

COVER DESIGN:
Michael Baumber

PUBLISHER:
Steve O'Hara

PUBLISHING DIRECTOR:
Dan Savage

COMMERCIAL DIRECTOR:
Nigel Hole

ADVERTISING MANAGER:
Sue Keily

ADVERTISING EXECUTIVE:
Craig Amess

MARKETING MANAGER:
Charlotte Park

ISBN:
978-1-911639-00-8

PUBLISHED BY:
Mortons Media Group Ltd,
Media Centre, Morton Way,
Horncastle,
Lincolnshire,
LN9 6JR.
Tel: 01507 529529

PRINTED BY:
William Gibbons and Sons,
Wolverhampton

MORTONS
MEDIA GROUP LTD

DARLINGTON: FROM LOCOMOTION TO IEPS

Darlington's rail legacy lives on, nearly 200 years after *Locomotion* took to the rails.

Darlington is renowned for being the cradle of the world's railways and it continues to play a vital role in the history of the UK rail industry.

When *Locomotion* made its pioneering run in 1825, no one could have envisaged that, 200 years later, countries from all around the world would have embraced this technology, enabling whole swathes of the globe to be opened up to freight and passengers alike.

Ironically, it was coal, not people, that became the driving force behind the invention of the railways, with mine owners looking for an efficient alternative to canals to be able to move coal around the country and to the docks for export.

Everybody has heard of *Rocket*, and it is almost as famous as *Flying Scotsman*, but *Locomotion* was the real railway pioneer, something that has the opportunity to be emphasised in 2025 with the bicentenary of the Stockton & Darlington Railway, which promises to be an event not to be missed.

Although much of the original route is in a woeful condition, plans are afoot to rectify this in time for 2025, with part of it being turned into a cycle route.

Locomotion may be but a distant memory, but Darlington is still at the forefront of rail engineering. The massive Hitachi factory at Newton Aycliffe is responsible for the new generation of East Coast and Great Western express trains, along with the successful class 385s for ScotRail. In one respect, the wheel has turned full circle, for it was the UK that supplied Japan with its first trains! Hitachi is confident that more orders will come its way once the current contracts finish.

Locomotive building of a slightly different variety, but still very exciting, is in the shape of the A1 Steam Locomotive Trust, which built the famous *Tornado* in 2008 and is now in the process of building 2007 *Prince of Wales*, which will, in due course, be followed by a K4.

The main station at Darlington is a work of beauty. It's just a pity that it is often overlooked in favour of York station, a few miles south along the East Coast Main Line. The latter station may well be bigger, but Darlington is well worth a visit, as is the nearby North Road station, along with the adjacent Head of Steam railway museum, a facility that was once threatened with closure.

Thankfully, the council was forced into retreat once it became clear that local people had other ideas. This historic facility is now only open part time, but at least it's still open.

One of the lesser-known 'locomotives' to be built in Darlington is the brick A4, located a short distance outside the city centre. Not greeted with universal admiration when it was unveiled, it has become an integral part of the area and certainly helped generate a lot of press interest at the time of its construction.

So, what of the future? There is every indication that Darlington will continue to play an important role in the UK's rail history for many more years to come and that the 2025 celebrations will be a great success, if all the plans currently being worked up come to fruition.

FROM TOP LEFT CLOCKWISE:

On June 11, 2019, 'Pacer' unit 142084 sets off from its station stop at Heighington, forming the 2D36 12:11 Bishop Auckland to Saltburn. GORDON EDGAR

60163 *Tornado* heads across the historic Skerne bridge at North Road on May 11, 2019. This much modified bridge has its origins in the Stockton and Darlington Railway, opened in 1825, and has appeared on the £5 Bank of England note. GORDON EDGAR

31285 crossing Wolsingham Bridge on April 21, 2018. JOHN ASKWITH

2007 *Prince of Wales* is rolled out at Darlington in June 2018. DAVID ELLIOTT

3170 makes its way towards Embsay on October 19, 2018. JOHN HUNT

Chapter 1

How it all BEGAN

How Darlington cemented its place in the history books as the world's most important railway town.

60163 *Tornado* heads across the historic Skerne bridge at North Road on May 11, 2019. This much modified bridge has its origins in the Stockton and Darlington Railway. GORDON EDGAR

BRITISH

Locomotion No.1 at the Head of Steam museum in Darlington. DARLINGTON BOROUGH COUNCIL

Unlike traditional railway towns, which were born out of railway companies developing greenfield sites and providing staff with housing, churches and schools, Darlington was already heavily industrialised by 1825, with the quality of its linen industry being well known. Its location on the Great North Road and renowned market also made it attractive to industrial investment.

The growth in the manufacture of wool and linen in the 1830s saw an explosion in the town's population from the 7500 inhabitants of 1825. These businesses were the foundations of the wealth generated by the Pease family and it was they, along with Quaker colleagues, who proved instrumental in bringing the railway to Darlington.

By the 1850s housing for railway employees had been created, with the S&DR staff living in a railway village at Hopetown and the GNER staff living near Bank Top station. The former's population was around 250, with the latter nearer 1000. It's interesting to note that these villages were not built by the railway companies as a way of looking after their staff, but by housing speculators looking for a good return on their investment.

The GNER did, however, build a church to serve its workers, the first stone being laid during a ceremony in September 1847, with the church opening three years later. It is reported that the rail workers did not always appreciate the church bells being rung if they were in bed following a night shift!

The houses provided for staff were of the basic two-up, two-down variety with a tiny yard and outside lavatory. Other 'worker villages' sprung up to house those associated with auxiliary roles to the railway. Further out of town, in more pleasant gentrified surroundings, middle class housing was created for the more educated rail worker, such as designers etc. These tenants benefited from gardens, among other enhanced amenities, denied to the staff from the working class estates.

Edward Pease, wealthy local wool merchant whose input helped develop the railway.

Ask most people who the father of the railways was and most will probably give the name of George Stephenson. However, it was the businesslike vision of Edward Pease (1767-1858) that saw the Stockton and Darlington Railway come to fruition.

Opening on September 27, 1825, the S&DR had been planned for many years prior to this momentous occasion, with Pease playing a pivotal role, for it was he who had the foresight to conclude that the movement of coal from the Durham pits to the River Tees by endless and slow trains of packhorses was unsustainable. Edward Pease was a man of many talents, and someone who is still held in significant reverence by those in the region today. Not only was he a Quaker, but also coal owner, merchant and manufacturer of wool. He was also well known as a philanthropist, no doubt influenced by his Quaker faith.

The lead up to the opening of the S&DR was fraught with many difficulties, the first being whether the railway should be built at all, for there were many who took the view that a canal would be a better option. This opinion gained considerable traction and in 1767 a survey was commissioned to determine the best way to construct a canal from the Auckland coalfield to the River Tees, the proposal seeing the canal join the river near Stockton.

Respected canal engineer James Brindley was approached to conduct the survey, a task that was given to his son-in-law Robert Whitworth. The survey was carried out during the summer of 1768, being finally presented to Darlington's business community in October of the following year. The report concluded the most viable route would be from Winston on the River Tees to Stockton-on-Tees, via Cockerton, a village on the outskirts of Darlington. It would see branches diverging off the main route, to serve Croft, Piercebridge and Yarm. In total this equated to just over 33 miles and the estimated cost of construction was put at £64,000. However, the period between the commissioning of the report and its delivery had seen the economic climate change for the worse, resulting in the proposals being shelved.

Nothing more was heard of such a proposal until around 30 years later, when the unsuitability of the River Tees as a navigable river was again beginning to cause much frustration among the region's business leaders. The main problems with the River Tees were its meandering route and susceptibility to silting. These factors meant that large vessels had to use the less convenient, and smaller, ports at Newport and Cargo Fleet. With frustration beginning to boil over, it was decided in 1805 to create the Tees Navigation Company. This new organisation immediately began work on a series of improvements, the most significant being the opening of Mandale Cut, which reduced the distance between Stockton and the mouth of the Tees by just over two miles. In 1810, the same year that the new short cut opened, thoughts began to turn once again to constructing a canal, but this time consideration was also given to constructing a railway instead.

This railway proposal was greeted with incredulity and not without a degree of humour, for a line of such length had never been built in the region. At this stage, pressure was still being applied to favour the construction of a new canal, pressure that was unrelenting for many years after a railway was first considered. Nevertheless, on the proviso that whatever method of transport was to eventually succeed would make a worthwhile return for its investors, a survey was commissioned to determine once and for all if a railway or canal should triumph.

Engineer and well-known canal builder John Rennie was tasked with carrying out the survey, presenting his findings in 1813. Unsurprisingly, he favoured the construction of a canal along the original route that had been outlined almost half a century previously. However, the intervening years had seen the estimated cost of constructing the canal shoot up to just under £206,000. It was to be another year before Rennie's report was to be considered and in 1815, the project was once again abandoned on cost grounds. This time, however, the time lapse between shelving and reviving the plans for a canal was but three years, when, in 1818, Stockton merchant Christopher Tennant financed yet another survey, but this time for a more direct route that would avoid Darlington and Yarm.

This new proposal was met with great enthusiasm from fellow merchants, even though the cost was little different from the estimate put forward for the construction of Rennie's canal. It's worth noting that Edward Pease was also present at the public meeting where Tennant announced his intentions, but had no vote. Those merchants located around Darlington were extremely upset at the prospect of being cast aside from the route of the proposed new canal and had no hesitation in letting their feelings be known to anyone of any influence. Main opponents to Tennant's route included land owner Thomas Meynell and his steward Jeremiah Cairns, the latter proving extremely useful in steering the mindset of many business leaders away from canals and towards the possibility of constructing a railway. Cairns was, via marriage, related to engineer George Overton, someone who had a long history of constructing Welsh colliery tramways. Concerned that the new proposal for a canal was gaining momentum, Cairns wrote to Overton expressing his opinion that a rail link would be more beneficial, both in terms of efficiency and financial returns. Overton was naturally interested and agreed with many of Cairn's opinions, so much so that Cairns shared Overton's letters with Richard Miles, a Yarm businessman with interests in the slate and timber trades.

These letters proved to be the catalyst that kick-started the serious proposal to throw the canal plans out once and for all, with Miles suggesting that a railway would be the ideal solution to difficulties encountered by merchants in moving their goods up to now. It was slowly dawning on other businessmen from Darlington and surrounding areas that maybe the fixation with canals was not a healthy one, with Edward Pease heaping much praise on Miles for his foresight and entrepreneurial attitude.

In September 1818, a committee was assembled to consider the advantages that a railway would have over a canal and the proposed route. It was decided to instruct Overton to carry out a survey that had to be done in secret, as some business leaders were hesitant about using any other engineer but Rennie. Being understandably enthusiastic about the prospect of a railway being

Locomotive *Derwent* at the Head of Steam Museum in Darlington.
DARLINGTON BOROUGH COUNCIL

The corporate seal of the Stockton & Darlington Railway Company. Its Latin motto reads: 'At private risk for public service'.

built, Overton completed his survey in a little over two weeks and while he concluded that the construction of a canal was feasible, it would be more sensible to construct a railway from Etherley colliery to Stockton, via Darlington. Overton estimated the cost of constructing the railway at £124,000. Thus, the Stockton and Darlington Railway was born, with the title being officially applied to the project from September 21, when a railway committee was also created.

In order to comply with Parliamentary rules, the committee authorised the Parliamentary notice in early September, with an additional application being made for an act that would enable the construction of a canal or railway having to be made before the end of the month. All was not, however, plain sailing for the railway supporters, as some advocates of the canal option began to get cold feet, insisting that Rennie be allowed to pass his professional judgment on the project. Rennie rejected the request and Robert Stevenson, who had successfully completed a number of rail projects in Scotland, carried out the survey instead. It was all too little, too late and Stevenson's survey had minimal impact on subsequent events. Without a detailed report from either Rennie or Stevenson, Overton's initial report was presented to potential investors during a meeting at Darlington Town Hall in November 1818. Although Rennie had turned down the invitation to carry out the latest survey, he did state that both modes of transport had their benefits and drawbacks. The gist of his statement was that canals were better when the amount of goods carried were equal in both directions, but railways were preferable when the balance was unequal.

In the end, the railway supporters won the day, no doubt helped by speaker Edward Pease who said that there would be a return of 5% on an investment of £120,000, his calculations being based on money generated by tolls from the coal road connecting West Auckland to Darlington. This was music to the ears of the local business community and so an application to Parliament was lodged for an act allowing the construction of a railway along the whole length of the route.

Within a month, a prospectus had been drawn up and issued, it being drawn up by Joseph Pease, son of Edward. The prospectus carried the grand title of 'Prospectus for making a public railway from the collieries near Auckland to Darlington, Yarm and Stockton, for the supply of the South and East parts of the County of Durham and the North Riding of Yorkshire with coals, and for the general conveyance of merchandise. To be established by subscription, in shares of one hundred pounds each.'

The prospect of such an economic upturn raised people's hopes to almost fever pitch and within just one week £25,000 had been subscribed; at the same time, the estimate for constructing the line had been reduced to £113,000. The subscription list closed on December 24, 1818 and by this time £80,000 of shares were held by Quakers.

Although things were looking decidedly positive, the project still had to overcome a number of hurdles, not least getting the S&DR bill passed. On the first attempt, which took place in April 1819, it suffered a narrow defeat of 106 votes to 93. The reasons for this defeat are thought to revolve around opposition from the Earl of Darlington and the Earl of Eldon, who were concerned as to what damage could be inflicted on their land by the construction of a rail line.

The Earl of Eldon eventually dropped his opposition to the scheme once a satisfactory deal had been reached regarding compensation for his loss, but his Darlington counterpart was not so easily swayed, and remained adamant that the railway should not encroach on his land. As a result, a second survey was carried out by Overton, with the result that the railway's route would now be diverted around the Earl of Darlington's land. The new route would see a line comprising of a total of 37 miles, which was nine miles shorter than the line originally envisaged, including branches.

The untimely death of King George III in January 1820 delayed the second bill. This delay proved fortuitous for the line's promotors, as it enabled them to buy more time and approach Overton with a view to him revising the plans to establish a shorter route. August 1820 saw this latest survey completed and it was this third version that was submitted to Parliament.

By this time the cost had been reduced even further to £92,000 and on April 19, 1821 the first S&DR Act received the Royal assent. Surprisingly it was not the first such Act to be passed by Parliament that century, but the 21st. The Act gave authority for £100,000 of capital to be raised, 80% of it in the form of shares, with the remaining balance by way of a loan.

The passing of the bill had been a close-run thing, as it was but a whisker away from not complying with the order that four-fifths of the share capital must be subscribed before the bill reached the committee stage. With only days to spare before the deadline, it was discovered that there was a shortfall of £7000. This induced panic among some of the backers and only the calm hand of Edward Pease saved the day when he, without hesitation, subscribed the

ANNO PRIMO & SECUNDO

GEORGII IV. REGIS.

****

Cap. xliv.

An Act for making and maintaining a Railway or Tramroad from the River *Tees* at *Stockton*, to *Witton Park Colliery*, with several Branches therefrom, all in the County of *Durham*.

[19th *April* 1821.]

WHEREAS the making and maintaining of a Railway or Tramroad, for the Passage of Waggons and other Carriages from the River *Tees*, at or near *Stockton*, in the County of *Durham*, to *Witton Park Colliery*, in the Township of *Witton*, in the said County of *Durham*, with Five collateral Branches from the said Railway or Tramroad; one of them commencing in the Township of *Egglescliffe*, and terminating at or near *Yarm Bridge*, in the said County of *Durham*; another of such collateral Branches commencing at or near *Lowson's Slack*, and terminating at or near *Northgate Bridge*, in the Township of *Darlington*, in the said County of *Durham*; another of such collateral Branches commencing at or near *Brussleton*, in the Township of *St. Helen's Auckland*, in the said County of *Durham*, and terminating at or near *Coundon* Turnpike Gate, in the Township of *Coundon*, in the said County of *Durham*; another of the said collateral Branches commencing at or near *Norlees House*, in the Township of *West Auckland*, and terminating at or near

[*Local.*] 15 *R* *Evenwood*

A copy of the Act of Parliament empowering the building of the Stockton & Darlington Railway. ROBIN JONES

Phoenix Pit at Etherley, near the northern terminus of the Stockton & Darlington Railway.

£7000 himself – this was in addition to the £3000 that he had already subscribed. It is little known that the Quaker community as a whole played a huge financial part in making the S&DR a success, with Darlington being known as 'The Quaker Town' and the S&DR earning the name of 'The Quaker Line'. The Quaker influence went way beyond Darlington and Quakers from other parts of the UK; many related to Edward Pease via marriage invested considerable sums in the new railway. Due to the Pease family having invested heavily in the S&DR, they played the dominant role with regard to policy and management structures.

The early 1820s saw Pease take a great deal of personal interest in the scheme, having always favoured a railway over the construction of a canal. His main concern was that the railway should be beneficial to his woollen mills in Darlington, which would see his transportation costs reduced considerably. Once this was assured he was much relieved. It was during this period that George Stephenson first became involved with the project. Many know of his *Rocket* locomotive, but few know of his background. Born in June 1781 in a house near Wylam Colliery, where his father Robert was the pumping engine's fireman, his first job was at Dewley Burn Colliery in 1794 and comprised him removing foreign material, such as stones, from newly dug coal. From there he moved around a number of local collieries, including becoming an assistant fireman to his father, before eventually becoming engine-wright at High Pit Colliery at Killingworth. His experience and success in constructing locomotives and creating colliery railways soon brought him to the attention of Edward Pease.

A meeting between the two railway giants took place in Darlington during April 1821, during the course of which Pease was very impressed with Stephenson's attitude and work ethic, describing him as honest, sensible, modest and unpretending, and the meeting marked the start of a long-lasting friendship between the two men. The very next day Pease wrote to Stephenson asking him if he would consider becoming the surveyor and engineer for the line's construction. Stephenson replied that although he would be happy to accept, he would not, due to pressure of other work, be able to devote himself full time to the role.

One of the first things that Stephenson did was dissuade Pease from his notion of using horses to haul wagons along the railway, instead insisting that steam locomotives would offer considerable advantages over any animal. Pease was already coming around to this way of thinking so did not need much persuasion to accept Stephenson's recommendation, especially after he informed Pease that a locomotive was equivalent to at least 50 horses. As if to hammer the point home, Pease was invited to Killingworth Colliery to see Stephenson's locomotive in action. Upon watching the locomotive in action hauling heavy coal wagons, Pease was immediately smitten with the locomotive and is on record as having said that there would be "no difficulty in laying a railway from London to Edinburgh on which wagons would travel and take the mail at the rate of 20 miles per hour." An equally enthusiastic George Stephenson encouraged Pease's enthusiasm by saying: "You will live to see the day when the railways will supersede almost all other methods of conveyance in the country – when mail coaches will go by railway and railways will became the great highway for the king and all his subjects. The time is coming when it will be cheaper for a working man to travel on a railway than to walk on foot."

The next task to be completed was the creation of a smaller management committee, this comprising of 14 of the line's major subscribers. Pease, along with his son Joseph, were elected on to a sub committee that had the authority to award contracts. Surprisingly, and perhaps indicative that the company, although not Edward Pease, still thought that the use of horse-drawn wagons was a distinct possibility, the seal depicted a horse hauling coal wagons. Prior to the line opening, Edward Pease handed over his interest in the railway to Joseph.

Stephenson was asked to resurvey the route that Overton had initially surveyed, due to the initial survey being conducted with a view that the envisaged route would not be used by locomotives, but by horse-drawn wagons. The faith that was placed in Stephenson's opinions and ability saw

Brusselton engineman cottages, October 10, 2014. R A BARBER

Brusselton incline west, October 10, 2014. R A BARBER

Brusselton Incline bridge, April 14, 1968. R GOAD/ARPT

Brusselton Incline west abandoned, looking east, undated. J W ARMSTRONG/ARPT

Overton pushed out of the equation, with his name being subsequently banished in Darlington.

Having accepted the post of line surveyor in August 1821, for a fee of £140 he also requested that someone should accompany him who was on friendly terms with the landowners over whose land the railway would travel. Once again, fortune was on the side of Stephenson, and the dry weather enabled the survey to be concluded within two weeks, considerably quicker than had been originally envisaged. Among his assistants for this exercise was his 18-year-old son Robert, this survey marking his first foray into the world of railway engineering. The report was finished in the following January and followed every foot of Overton's original plan of the route, complete with Stephenson's modifications.

Work on constructing the route commenced on May 13, 1822, with rapid progress being made. The first rails to be laid were on May 23, near Stockton's St John's Well level crossing. This momentous occasion was marked by a grand ceremony performed by S&DR chairman Thomas Meynell and accompanied by much bell ringing from a nearby church.

The six-mile section of route between its starting point at Witton Park Colliery, near the River Tyne, and New Shildon was relatively hilly, due to it traversing the two high watersheds known as the Etherley and Brusselton ridges. Between the two ridges was the valley of the River Gaunless, which acted as a tributary of the River Wear. Such was the severity of gradient along this section of route that the use of locomotives was never even contemplated. The remaining 20 miles to Stockton via Darlington was much more forgiving, being relatively level, with the stiffest gradient being 1:104. The first section would be worked by stationary steam engine, something that Overton had also envisaged, but, unlike Overton, who planned to use horse power for the remainder of the route, Stephenson saw no benefit in such an idea, opting for the far superior steam locomotive. The stationary engine was located at Phoenix Row at the foot of Etherley Ridge, with wagons being worked up and down the incline via way of a pair of inclined planes, powered by said engine.

Witton Park Colliery was located midway between Witton Park House and Witton Park Farm and, today, all traces of its historical past have been swept away and one would never know there had ever been a colliery there, never mind the world's first railway.

A short distance beyond Etherley, the railway breached the River Gaunless by way of the world's first cast iron railway bridge. This Stephenson-designed structure originally comprised three spans but following storm damage in 1824, an additional span was added to the bridge. It had a relatively short life, closing to rail traffic in 1856 after the Brusselton inclines were bypassed. However, it proved not to be the end, as in 1901 the West Auckland section of route was reinstated in connection with the reopening of Brusselton Colliery. By this time it had been decided that the cast iron bridge was no longer fit for purpose and it was replaced by a stone structure by the S&DR's successor, the North Eastern Railway. The original cast iron bridge does live on though, as it was claimed by the National Railway Museum, one of the few items to have survived from the line.

Stephenson was very critical of Overton's plans to build a route over the "dangerously steep" Brusselton west incline, choosing instead to build the line on a far gentler gradient that followed the northern slope of the ridge. This proved a wise decision and Stephenson's summit was located just a few yards from that which was originally planned by Overton. Once over the summit, the line made an immediate descent to the foot of the ridge. Stephenson was keen, knowing the limitations of steam locomotives, to ensure, where possible, that the route to Stockton was on a gradual falling gradient, with as many straight sections of track as possible. Problems with laying track were encountered at Miers Flat due to it being made up of a low-lying marshy area. To overcome this challenge, Stephenson had to bring in hundreds of tons of earth and dump it into the bog until enough soil had been imported for him to create a firm foundation for the railway to pass over. This method of construction was to be used by Stephenson again during the construction of the Liverpool and Manchester Railway for the section across Chat Moss. Upon reaching Oaktree Junction, Stephenson opted for the route to Stockton set out by Overton, due to the latter's decision to make the route relatively straight and not a meandering one. Overton's initial plans for the line were heavily criticised by Stephenson, who could see no real reason for Overton wanting to create embankments that would have involved importing many tons of spoil by cart, when they could be created by using the soil dug out from nearby cuttings, being transported to site in wagons running on temporary rails. The line was, in essence, a single line which included numerous passing loops in order that capacity could be maximised.

A presentation model of the Gaunless Bridge was made for the North Eastern Railway in 1875 to mark the 50th anniversary of the opening of the Stockton & Darlington Railway. It is now displayed in the Science Museum in London.

A special sub-committee was created to establish what material would best be suited for the rails that were to be used on the line. Barring the earthworks, the rails were the biggest item of expenditure, so it was critical that the right material was chosen. The committee visited many rail and tramways to examine the various types of rail in use at the time, in order that an educated decision could be reached. It was about this time that wrought iron had been invented, which was fortunate indeed as it was far superior to the cast iron that had been used for rails up until this time. Not only was wrought iron stronger and lighter, it had the significant added advantage of being far less prone to developing fractures, something that was especially important when it was to suffer the daily punishment of hammer blows

The original rail bridge still remains at Shildon Yard, although it is now converted into a walkway. Pictured on October 20, 1974. R GOAD/ARPT

from heavily laden wagons. Until now, the use of wrought iron rails had been severely limited due to them being of simple square sections, making them only really suitable for narrow gauge mine tramways. By 1821 the Bedlington iron works had perfected a method that could produce wrought iron rails in 20ft lengths. Stephenson was not slow in recognising how this new invention could revolutionise the railways and made strong representations to the S&DR rail sub-committee, urging them to make best use of this new technology. The committee partially heeded his advice by ordering wrought iron rails for two-thirds of the line and cast iron rails for the remainder, including the loops. As ever, cost was behind this decision, with wrought iron rails costing just over £12 a ton, compared to £6 for cast iron, although the significant difference in weight between the two materials made the cost per mile more or less the same. This made the S&DR the first railway to make large use of wrought iron rails. When finances improved the decision was made to replace the cast iron rails with wrought iron ones, albeit of a more robust specification in order to cope with the increase in traffic along the route and the heavier loads being carried.

Such was the success of the new line that in 1832 just over 19 miles between Brusselton Bank and Stockton had to

MAIN LINE BRANCHES

The S&DR's main line had a number of branches to serve the numerous collieries and coal depots in the vicinity.

The Darlington coal depot branch diverged from the main line near North Road station and opened on the same day as the main line.

The Yarm coal depot branch was just over a mile in length and left from the main line at a spot near the original Yarm station. The first coal train to traverse the branch line was on October 11, 1825, shortly after the main line had opened, with the branch being officially opened to traffic six days later.

Passenger trains along the branch commenced in October 1826. This was a quirky arrangement, where the horse-drawn passenger services took the branch line, before rejoining the main line. This odd practice only ceased in 1833, once steam locomotives ruled supreme. The branch closed in 1871.

The 2½ mile Black Boy branch came off the main line at Shildon Junction and was constructed to serve two collieries of the same name, the name originating from a local pub. The first colliery was named Old Black Boy, with the second being called simply Black Boy, being renamed Old Black Boy when the former mine closed in 1830.

The latter colliery continued in use for another three decades.

The branch comprised steep inclines and so had to make use of stationary steam engines located at the summit of High Shildon, which operated over an incline of 1-in-20. Unbelievably, these steep inclines were originally worked by horses until 1828, due to the stationary engines still being under construction. These only lasted in service for seven years before being replaced by more reliable stationary engines supplied by Timothy Hackworth.

The branch proved of great benefit for the local industry and new collieries sprung up along its route, many of them also being named Black Boy, which could make things very confusing from a railway operations point of view.

Opening in 1829, the Croft Depot branch was just over three miles long and diverged from the main line near Albert Hill and a short distance beyond the River Skerne bridge. It served the Croft coal depot and wharf, which were located on the banks of the River Tees. Opening on October 27, 1829 it was soon thriving with traffic from numerous coal mines. Between its opening and 1833, the branch line also saw a horse-drawn passenger service.

Agreement to construct the Haggerleases branch was only granted on condition that the S&DR relinquished its proposal to build a branch line from Norlees House to Evenwood Lane. This abandoned plan would have seen a branch line of just over two miles, whereas the Haggerleases line would reach a length of just under five miles and followed the path of the River Gaunless throughout its route.

The branch broke away from the main line just north of where it crossed the river. After the first half a mile had been built in 1824 construction came to a halt for a number of years as a result of financial difficulties.

Work did not recommence until the summer of 1828, with the whole branch opening for service in late 1830.

As with the other branches already mentioned, the branch line acted as a catalyst for the local economy and within two decades the branch had 12 stubs emanating from it, serving a dozen collieries.

Such was the rugged terrain that the line followed that a skew arch bridge, thought to be only the second such bridge to have been built in the UK, had to be constructed for the line to cross the River Gaunless.

This was obviously far from a straightforward engineering feat, so in order to ensure that there was little chance of mistakes happening, it was decided to construct a full-size model, made out of wood, in a nearby field. The stone bridge, which was designed by Thomas Storey and built by James Wilson, opened in 1830 and remained in use until 1963.

Parkside accommodation bridge on the 1829 branch to Croft. JW ARMSTRONG/ARPT

be doubled to be able to cope with the amount of traffic now being generated. This not only involved the laying of another track, but the widening of cuttings to be able to accommodate it.

George Stephenson became the driving force in ensuring that the 4ft 8½in gauge became the standard gauge for the new railway, the same gauge that was used at Killingworth. At the time there was no standard gauge and each colliery decided on its own gauge.

ON TO MIDDLESBROUGH

Very shortly after the opening of the Stockton and Darlington Railway, it soon became increasingly clear that the Stockton coaling staithes were incapable of dealing with large ships. At this point it was decided that the best course of action would be to extend the S&DR to either Haverton Hill, situated on the north bank of the river, or Middlesbrough on the southern bank. After a survey of both routes had been conducted, it was decided to opt for the Middlesbrough route. This was primarily because it was the most direct and, most importantly, the cheapest of the two routes. The four-mile extension opened to traffic in December 1830, with Timothy Hackworth's steam locomotive *The Globe* hauling the first train.

In what many considered a fit of pique, the Tees Navigation Authority demanded that river traffic should not be interrupted by the installation of bridge piers. This caused some concern with the S&DR engineers, with plans for a cast iron or wrought iron bridge being rejected. Eventually, it was decided to break with convention and build not only the world's first railway suspension bridge, but the first railway bridge to be constructed across a navigable river. The cost of the 412ft bridge was just over £2000, with a main span that measured 281ft and weighed in at 111 tons. Such lightweight construction caused many to doubt if it would be capable of carrying heavy coal trains, so a number of tests were carried out, with alarming results. When a train of nearly 70 tons was placed on the bridge, the structure underwent a severe deflection, causing the couplings to snap and then roll back and forth, rather like a pendulum. A temporary solution was to use couplings that maintained a distance of 27ft between batches of four wagons, but this was obviously never going to be a long-term solution, with some drivers refusing to cross the bridge while on the footplate, instead choosing to set the locomotive in motion, jump off and run ahead across the bridge, before jumping back on their loco when it reached the other side. With no realistic solution to the troubles at hand, the only action that was possible had to be taken, and that involved demolishing and replacing the bridge, something that happened in 1844, the new bridge being to a more conventional design by Robert Stephenson.

This new structure comprised five cast iron girders that were supported by stone piers. The story doesn't end there though, as this second bridge was renewed in 1907, although its successor did make use of the stone piers.

The extension to Middlesbrough also allowed the S&DR to open a locomotive works at Middlesbrough, this opening in 1842 and becoming known as The Tees Engine Works in 1844. Commencing with the next decade, it became the main works for the construction of S&DR locomotives, as well as diversifying into making equipment for mines etc.

The Middlesbrough extension saw a mass expansion in the amount of coal carried and in 1831 the S&DR conveyed a respectable 152,000 tons, but just two years later this figure had reached an astronomical 336,000 tons; this saw a significant drop in the cost of coal.

Cheapside in Shildon: a view of the Black Boy wagon way looking south, March 26, 1998. R A BARBER

Black Boy wagon way ran through Cheapside – a view looking north, October 22, 1996. R GOAD/ARPT

Cheapside: another view of the Black Boy wagon way looking north, taken March 5, 1967. R GOAD/ARPT

A portrait of Timothy Hackworth.

RIGHT: The late artist Ronald Embleton's depiction of *Locomotion No. 1* passing a stagecoach on the opening day of the Stockton & Darlington Railway.

A limited passenger service operated along the line and proved popular due to the poor state of the roads. This also encouraged people to use the track as a public footpath and the problem got so bad that a policeman had to be stationed near the main access point to try and prevent this. As a result, it was far from uncommon for those wishing to travel to Middlesbrough, and who had missed the last passenger train, to jump on a following coal train – sometimes even the footplate itself – to avoid being charged with trespassing on the railway.

It was the ingenious Timothy Hackworth who put forward an innovative design for staithes that could allow rail wagons to discharge their load directly into the hull of the ship. Another important factor was that Hackworth's staithes kept the coal chunks from breaking up, which was most appreciated by colliery owners as coal prices were based on the size of the coal. Six such staithes were constructed, with the first loaded ship departing in December 1831.

With construction of the line progressing at a rapid pace, the question of motive power became an urgent priority. Surprisingly, even at this late stage, the options included horse power as well as locomotives, or even a combination of the two. The reason for this seemingly luddite view was that there was still a lingering doubt as to whether horse power was superior to a steam locomotive. Things swung in the favour of steam power as a result of a vast increase in the price of horse feed, brought about by the Napoleonic wars. Mine owners began to slowly realise that it made more financial sense to use a form of traction that ran on the material that they produced. In the end, after Edward Pease had paid another visit to Killingworth to watch George Stephenson's locomotive at work, steam traction was chosen to work the line. The next decision to be made was who would build the locomotives. It was at this point that Stephenson took the plunge and founded a company that was capable of locomotive construction, the Newcastle-based firm being registered in 1823. Edward Pease became a partner in the company along with George Stephenson, his son Robert and Michael Longridge. This became the world's first purpose-built loco works. In July 1824 the new firm, which bore Robert Stephenson's name, was approached and invited to tender for the construction of two locomotives for the new railway, with an order being placed in September, each engine costing £500 each. The two locomotives were named *Locomotion No.1* and *Hope*, being built to a design based on George Stephenson's Killingworth engines. The company also built the two stationary winding engines that were to be used on the Brusselton and Etherley inclines.

Hackworth's cottages in Shildon, May 28, 1966. R GOAD/ARPT

Although based on the locomotives in use at the Killingworth Colliery, *Locomotion No.1* performed in a far superior way to the Killingworth locomotives. One of the main enhancements was the valve and drive gear. However, things did not go smoothly, for during the construction of the two locomotives in 1824, Robert Stephenson resigned from the company and became the resident engineer to the Columbian Mining Association in South America. The reason for his sudden departure is unclear, but it is thought that a disagreement with his father lay at the bottom of it. This departure saw the company descend into near chaos, with deadlines for the delivery of locomotives missed. A clearly frustrated Edward Pease informed Robert Stephenson that the business was suffering terribly in his absence and if he did not return forthwith it would undoubtedly close.

It was around this time that Tyneside colliery engineer Timothy Hackworth joined the staff, where his engineering skills helped prove invaluable to the workshop and, indeed, he was charged with supervising the construction of *Locomotion No.1*. Upon the locomotive's completion in September 1825 it was, rather ironically, dragged from the works on three horse-drawn wagons and transported to the line at Aycliffe Road.

A stone memorial to mark the operation of the first passenger train stands in landscaped area in Byreley Road, Shildon, close to the former railway works. CHRIS MILNER

STOCKTON & DARLINGTON

RAILWAY COMPANY

Hereby give Notice,

THAT the FORMAL OPENING of their RAILWAY will take place on the 27th instant, as announced in the public Papers.—The Proprietors will assemble at the Permanent Steam Engine, situated below BRUSSELTON TOWER*, *about nine Miles West of* DARLINGTON, *at* 8 *o'clock, and, after examining their extensive inclined Planes there, will start from the Foot of the* BRUSSELTON *descending Plane, at* 9 *o'clock, in the following Order:*——

1. THE COMPANY'S LOCOMOTIVE ENGINE.
2. The ENGINE'S TENDER, with Water and Coals.
3. SIX WAGGONS, laden with Coals, Merchandize, &c.
4. The COMMITTEE, and other PROPRIETORS, in the COACH belonging to the COMPANY.
5. SIX WAGGONS, with Seats reserved for STRANGERS.
6. FOURTEEN WAGGONS, for the Conveyance of Workmen and others.

☞ *The WHOLE of the above to proceed to STOCKTON.*

7. SIX WAGGONS, laden with Coals, to leave the Procession at the DARLINGTON BRANCH.
8. SIX WAGGONS, drawn by Horses, for Workmen and others.
9. Ditto Ditto.
10. Ditto Ditto.
11. Ditto Ditto.

The COMPANY'S WORKMEN to leave the Procession at DARLINGTON, and DINE at that Place at ONE o'clock; excepting those to whom Tickets are specially given for YARM, and for whom Conveyances will be provided, on their Arrival at STOCKTON.

TICKETS will be given to the Workmen who are to dine at DARLINGTON, specifying the Houses of Entertainment.

The PROPRIETORS, and such of the NOBILITY and GENTRY as may honour them with their Company, will DINE precisely at THREE o'clock, at the TOWN-HALL, STOCKTON.—Such of the Party as may incline to return to DARLINGTON that Evening, will find Conveyances in waiting for their Accommodation, to start from the COMPANY'S WHARF there precisely at SEVEN o'clock.

The COMPANY take this Opportunity of enjoining on all their WORK-PEOPLE that Attention to *Sobriety* and *Decorum* which they have hitherto had the Pleasure of observing.

The COMMITTEE give this PUBLIC NOTICE, that all Persons who shall ride upon, or by the sides of, the RAILWAY, on Horseback, will incur the Penalties imposed by the Acts of Parliament passed relative to this RAILWAY.

* Any Individuals desirous of seeing the Train of Waggons descending the inclined Plane from ETHERLEY, and in Progress to BRUSSELTON, may have an Opportunity of so doing, by being on the RAILWAY at ST. HELEN'S AUCKLAND not later than Half-past Seven o'clock.

RAILWAY-OFFICE, *Sept. 19th*, 1825.

Notice of the opening of the Stockton & Darlington Railway.

THE LINE OPENS

In July of that year, George Stephenson had confidently announced that the line would be completed by September, with the management committee making the public announcement that the official opening of the Stockton and Darlington Railway would take place on September 27. Determined to make it a day to remember, the committee ensured that everyone within miles of the line knew about the date, resulting in many thousands attending.

Although the official opening was scheduled for September 27, a trial run, with *Locomotion No. 1* hauling the company carriage, took place on the previous evening. The locomotive was driven by James Stephenson – George's brother – with William Gowland as his fireman. Travelling in the carriage was Edward Pease and his sons Joseph, Henry and Edward, along with George Stephenson. This marked the first locomotive-hauled passenger carrying train, on a public railway, in the world.

Such was the excitement on the opening day that by 05.30 wagons that had had seats installed for passengers were already full. These wagons were horse-drawn from Darlington to the permanent steam engine located at the foot of Brusselton Tower. The opening ceremony commenced at 08.00, with some guests gathered at West Auckland and others congregated at Brusselton summit. The assembled guests observed the arrival of 12 laden coal wagons from Witton Park, and a wagon conveying flour, at the top of the ascending plane.

Departing from Shildon, the inaugural train consisted of a steam locomotive, 12 wagons of freight, the company carriage, 14 wagons conveying staff and six wagons for the use of 'normal' passengers. The latter were just coal wagons that had undergone a clean and had seats fitted. It's worth noting that the company carriage was, unsuprisingly, considered the most important vehicle in the train, with the 14 staff wagons considered the least prestigious. Unlike the coal wagons that had been fitted with seats to accommodate 'normals', the people conveyed in the staff wagons had to

A contemporary sketch of the first Stockton & Darlington train.

stand. The amount of time taken in terms of giving speeches etc., resulted in the inaugural train departing at 10am, an hour later than planned. Naturally, it was hauled by *Locomotion*, with George Stephenson driving, along with two of his brothers as firemen. Timothy Hackworth was the guard. It is a little-known fact that, such was the novelty of railways, trains had to be preceded by a man on horseback holding a red flag. One can imagine what George Stephenson thought of this arrangement! Indeed, a number of reports of the day's proceedings refer to *Locomotion* as a 'steam horse', reflecting the attitudes of the day. One report recalls how one observer fled in terror, following *Locomotion* blowing off steam, along with women and children. Gradually the terrified group gathered enough courage to return, but immediately fled again when *Locomotion's* safety valves lifted, fearing that the locomotive was about to explode. As the train made its way through the countryside, men on horseback in adjacent fields tried in vain to keep pace with the train that was now travelling at around 12mph.

Former Yarm coal depot, March 13,1955. R GOAD/ARPT

The eight-mile journey, which saw *Locomotion* tackle moderate gradients of 1-in-144 and 1-in-178 along the way, took two hours. The prolonged journey time was due to two derailments, caused by a wheel of one of the wagons conveying the engineers slipping on its axle. After it derailed for a second time, the decision was made to shunt the defective wagon out of the formation and dump it in one of the passing loops. During the shunt move, a passenger received a blow to his head, making him the first person to be injured during a public rail journey!

Just as Stephenson no doubt thought it couldn't get any worse, *Locomotion* came to a halt again, but this time due to a piece of lagging becoming entangled in one of the locomotive's feed pump valves. This saw the train halted for half an hour near Simpasture. The train eventually reached Darlington at 12.00, having taken an hour longer than envisaged and reaching an average speed of under 8mph. This disguises the fact that *Locomotion* did reach the heady speed of 15mph for a short stretch of almost two miles between Burtree Lane and Darlington, due in no short measure to the 1-in-134 falling gradient.

Prior to the opening train, a number of locals had been conveyed in wagons along parts of the route by carters who had been employed in its construction. An unofficial competition was held to see who could travel directly behind the inaugural train. A Mr J Lancaster won this hands down by strategically placing his wagon in a passing loop, thus allowing him to come out of the loop as soon as the train passed him and take up the much sought after lead position, a position he managed to maintain all the way to Stockton.

The inaugural train, which now comprised 34 vehicles, came to a halt near the branch serving the Darlington Coal depot, which is roughly where the site of Darlington North station now sits. By halting the train there, it enabled the rear six wagons, which contained coal, to be uncoupled and for horses to haul them to the branch terminus. Upon arrival, the wagons were emptied of their load, with the coal being distributed to the poor and needy. This proved to be an excellent PR exercise. Upon the train's arrival at Darlington, a number of ticket passengers disembarked, their places being quickly filled by others wishing to continue on the second stage of the trip.

Also at Darlington, two wagons were added to the formation for the conveyance of the Yarm brass band. It had been the original intention for the brass band to join the train at Yarm, space being made by workers vacating their seats. At Yarm, the train was brought to a stand in order that a number of coal wagons could be uncoupled, this also allowing all but two of the locals to come and witness the historic moment. The two absentees in question were two elderly ladies, who were thought to be too infirm to be able to make the effort.

Upon arrival at Darlington the opportunity was taken to coal and water *Locomotion*, before departure on the second stage of the journey, *Locomotion* departing Darlington at 12.38 and soon giving its passengers a spectacular view of the locality as it passed over the River Skerne.

As the train neared Stockton it ran near the road, allowing many hundreds of spectators to gather and watch *Locomotion* steam past at about 12mph. A stagecoach driver decided to enter the spirit of the occasion along this stretch of the route and challenged *Locomotion* to a race. The contrast in the two forms of traction was enormous; *Locomotion* hauling 600 passengers plus freight compared to a carriage powered by four horses, yet only able to convey six passengers. The number of horses and riders that greeted the train along the route also swiftly put paid to the notion by anti-railway land owners that steam locomotives would scare the animals. At this point it's worth sparing a thought for the poor rider in front, holding his red flag aloft, as *Locomotion* thundered past him and his steed. One can only guess as to his thoughts!

The last mile into Stockton was on a falling gradient, allowing Stephenson to take *Locomotion* up to the impressive

BRIDGE CONSTRUCTION

The construction of the bridge over the River Skerne became a source of friction between Stephenson and the proprietors, after the latter, having studied Stephenson's design for the bridge, asked him to liaise with architect Ignatius Bonomi. Stephenson was far from happy with this suggestion, perceiving it to be a slight on his ability.

Bonomi put forward a number of suggestions on how Stephenson's plans could be modified; in reality the plans put forward by Bonomi amounted to an almost total scrapping of Stephenson's proposals for the bridge.

The bridge was constructed in a classical, Italianate style, with a stone arch across the river and two smaller arches on the river bank to enable walkers to pass through. Stephenson had abandoned, very early on, his initial idea of an iron bridge due to the rising price of iron and difficulty in finding a contractor that was willing to carry out the work.

Doubling of the route in 1832 saw the bridge strengthened, with an additional section added to the north section.

speed of 15mph, although what this did for the well-being of *Locomotion* is open to debate, with reports claiming that by the time the train reached Stockton, the smokebox had taken on a distinctly orange glow. As if one accident was not enough, the second such incident occurred during this exuberant display of enginemanship, when a keelman, who had been clinging on to one of the wagons, lost his footing and was dragged beneath the wheels of the speeding train. Such was the severity of his injuries that amputation of his foot was the only remedy that could save him. Further sadness marked this otherwise happy occasion, due to Edward Pease being unable to attend following the death of his teenage son Isaac that same morning from consumption.

At 15.45 *Locomotion* reached the end of its 20-mile journey and blasted triumphantly into Stockton amid much cheering and waving. The 12 miles from Darlington had been achieved in three hours and seven minutes, giving an average speed of just under 4mph. As well as the exuberant crowd of well-wishers, a band played the national anthem, a peal of church bells rang out and there was even a 21-gun salute. Once the excitement had abated a little, the VIP passengers made their way to Stockton Town Hall for a feast, attended by 102 guests.

The passengers on board this first train can be divided into official and unofficial passengers. The former consisted of those that had been invited and included proprietors and their friends and family, along with people who had worked on the ground in constructing the line. The unofficial variety, and proving that fare-dodging is as old as the railways themselves, included chancers who jumped on and made themselves comfy on top of the coal in the open wagons, as well as those that decided to cling, rather dangerously, on to the sides sides of said wagons, this rather unusual practice leading to the keelman having his foot amputated. It is recorded that upon arrival at Darlington there were 84 passengers atop the coal wagons, before the wagons were shunted from the train.

For many years after locomotive-hauled passenger trains were introduced, it was not unusual for passengers to either travel without tickets, paying their fares direct to the driver or guard. Fares were, for the whole journey, 2s for first class and 1s 6d for second class.

Where fare-dodging was encountered, something that was relatively rare, those who had bought fares to cover only half the distance were placed in a separate carriage and should they refuse to disembark (hoping that they could travel the whole length of the line) the carriage was uncoupled and the errant passengers left behind. I'm sure that is something some train operators today would like to try!

Nineteenth-century Darlington artist John Dobbin's best-known work is the Opening of the Stockton & Darlington Railway, depicting the first train running over the Skerne Viaduct.

COAL EXPORTS

Much of the support from the public was due to the fact that the railway would enable the cost of coal to be reduced by one third and the prospect of the local economy booming. Indeed, within a very short time of its opening a contract was won for the shipment of 100,000 tons of coal to London annually for five years.

As a result the share price rocketed to £40 a share, with people clambering to purchase, but very few willing to sell.

The impact that the railway had on the movement of coal can be amply illustrated by the simple fact that in 1800 it was significantly cheaper to convey a ton of coal from Newcastle to London via sea than the 19 miles between Bishop Auckland and Stockton. By 1840 the cost of moving coal by rail had reached 1s 3d a ton, compared to 5d by road. This proved a catalyst for economic growth in the region, with many new collieries opening as a result. The export of coal really took off a year after the railway opened, with the first shipment occurring in January 1826, when the ship *Adamant* took 168 tons from Etherley colliery. Such was the demand that capacity was constantly at breaking point on the railway, with many recorded instances of loaded coal wagons causing congestion by blocking the rail route as they waited for ships to arrive. By June of the following year, the volume of coal shipped from Stockton had reached a staggering 18,588 tons. It would have been much more, but the limiting factor was the River Tees and its inability to accept large ships. This meant that ships of more than 100 tons were forbidden from departing the staithes fully loaded. It was to be another three years before the problem could be overcome, achieved by extending the line to a deeper riverside terminal at Middlesbrough. By 1833, 336,000 tons of coal was being carried by the railway. The movement of freight, primarily coal, was always the driving force behind constructing the railway, with the S&DR regarding the conveying

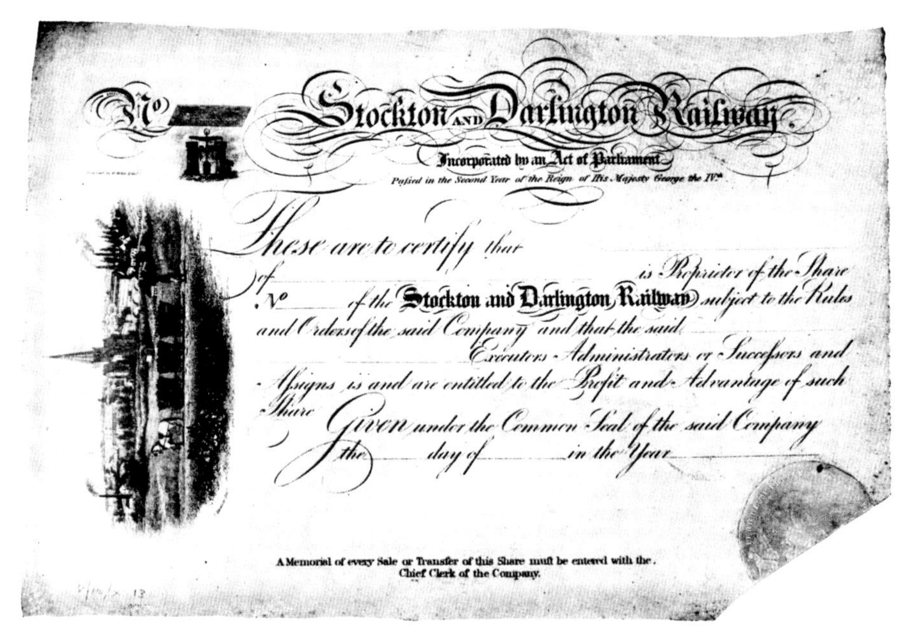

No. Stockton and Darlington Railway.
Incorporated by an Act of Parliament
Passed in the Second Year of the Reign of His Majesty George the IV th.
These are to certify that
of
is Proprietor of the Share
No of the Stockton and Darlington Railway subject to the Rules and Orders of the said Company and that the said
Executors Administrators or Successors and Assigns is and are entitled to the Profit and Advantage of such Share
Given under the Common Seal of the said Company the day of in the Year
A Memorial of every Sale or Transfer of this Share must be entered with the Chief Clerk of the Company.

A Stockton & Darlington Railway share certificate.

A scale model of *Locomotion No. 1* inside Deutsche Bahn's DB Museum in Nuremberg. ROBIN JONES

of passengers as very much a secondary activity, with the inclusion to do this an afterthought in the subsequently amended Act of Parliament. Taken aback by the demand for such a service, the proprietors were quick to realise the opportunities that lay ahead in introducing a passenger service and from October 10, 1825 commenced what it called 'The Company's Coach Experiment', with the passenger carriage making a daily return journey on Monday, Wednesday, Thursday and Friday with a one-way Stockton to Darlington service operating on Tuesdays and a one-way journey in the other direction on a Saturday. The poster announcing this great development became the world's first published passenger timetable.

Up until this time, the only public transport between the two locations was a single stagecoach that operated four times a week and was known to barely break even. In contrast to the great success of the railway in moving coal, the passenger carriage did not find favour with the public, being reported as rather uncomfortable due to the lack of suspension. It soon gained the nickname of the 'tub' and is reported to have resembled a caravan, not the most glamorous way for the public to travel. The underframe was constructed by Robert Stephenson's Newcastle works, with the body being built by a local coach builder. It lasted a mere 15 months in service before becoming a bothy for the workmen at Brusselton incline.

It was here that the coach was destroyed by fire, after igniting from a stray spark originating from a fire that had been started by the workers to keep warm. Not to be deterred, the S&DR replaced it the next year with a much improved vehicle.

Daniel Adamson coach house, Shildon. Picture taken April 14, 1968. R GOAD/ARPT

PASSENGER TRAIN

The first steam-hauled public passenger train made its journey from Stockton to Darlington at 07.00 on October 10, 1825, returning from Darlington at 15.00. The new improved vehicle was such a success that a second carriage was constructed and given the name 'Express'. This was very similar to the 'Experiment' carriage, but had enhanced comfort. Both carriages were owned by the S&DR, but leased to Richard Pickersgill.

This arrangement did not last long and a sea change was instigated by the landlords of a number of local pubs who, sensing that there was money to be made, announced that they planned to operate their own passenger services in direct competition with Pickersgill. At this point the S&DR cancelled its agreement with Pickersgill that had given him sole rights to operate passenger trains over the line. Thus began a period which saw passenger services contracted out to numerous operators who paid the S&DR 3d a mile for the privilege.

Between the line opening and November of the same year, only *Locomotion* was available for traffic, a situation not resolved until the delivery of *Hope* early that month, albeit much later than promised. The proprietors were obviously impressed with *Locomotion* as they soon placed an order for a further two engines, *Black Diamond* and *Diligence*, entering service consecutively in April and May 1826. This euphoria was not to last, as the proprietors were soon expressing their dissatisfaction with *Hope*, saying that it was delivered in a sub-standard condition and required the fitters to spend a week carrying out repairs

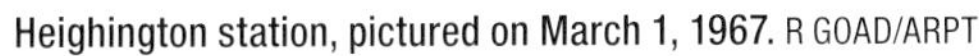

Heighington station, pictured on March 1, 1967. R GOAD/ARPT

The same station on July 11, 1994. R GOAD/ARPT

before it was deemed fit for service. This was only the start of a long list of loco failures, with *Locomotion* itself failing with a broken wheel just days after the opening. This saw it laid up in the works until mid-October.

Clearly frustrated with having locomotives out of service, for months at a time in some instances, the proprietors requested that Stephenson should not send any locomotive that had experimental apparatus fitted and only use equipment that had been tried and tested on other locomotives. Furthermore, it asked that a number of spare wheels be sent in case of further breakage.

In the intervening months things did not improve significantly, to the extent that the proprietors requested that Stephenson base a fitter at the depot to assist with maintaining the locomotives. *Locomotion* had a rather bad reputation among enginemen of the day, being infamous for its difficulty in driving. One driver went as far as to say that two-thirds of the footplate men could not drive *Locomotion* or her sisters without extreme difficulty. Robert Stephenson hit back by saying that a number of the problems encountered with the locomotives was due to the drivers not being suffiency skilled in loco handling, writing: "They (drivers) perhaps want improvement as much as the engines." Drivers received the princely sum of a farthing per ton per mile, but were required to pay the fireman as well as supply fuel. The company was pleased with this arrangement as it made financial sense from its perspective, but an unintended consequence was that it lay the system open to abuse. One of the main rules that was broken on a regular, almost habitual, basis was that of the 8mph speed limit. This was imposed in a bid to reduce the number of broken wheels, but was mainly ignored by all but the most subservient of drivers, especially if their train had suffered a delay en route. The record for the quickest return journey was held by driver Charles Tennison, who managed to cover the 90-mile round trip from Shildon to Stockton in just four-and-a-half hours. He was sacked for his efforts.

Footplate crews were known to play fast and loose with the rules during the early years of operation, with speeding, albeit not to the degree of driver Tennison, being commonplace – as was unofficial footplate riding by people hitching a lift.

Things took a serious turn in March 1828 when steam locomotive *Hope* suffered a catastrophic boiler explosion, killing driver John Gillespie in the process. Mr Gillespie became the first recorded instance of a death on an operational railway. Driver John Cree was killed in July of the same year, when *Locomotion*'s flue burst while it took on water at Aycliffe Lane. An investigation by Timothy Hackworth revealed that the explosions were as a result of drivers securing the safety valves with cord, so as to avoid the irritation of having to deal with escaping jets of steam, activated by the uneven track work. Seeing this, Hackworth installed a spring safety valve, which ended the

A Stockton & Darlington Railway coach preserved at Beamish Museum, its design resembling that of a stagecoach.

drivers' deadly practice.

Incidents involving steam locomotives continued to occur at regular intervals, including *Locomotion* overturning at New Shildon and Aycliffe Lane, hitting a donkey at Goosepool, its fireman losing a foot and colliding with wagons, once again at Goosepool.

The continuing catalogue of failures and all-round unreliability forced the ever-increasingly frustrated proprietors to resort to horse power for a number of the services. In fact, things had reached such a low point that serious consideration was given to abandoning the whole steam locomotive project and returning to horse-drawn trains as a permanent measure.

Such was the amount of coal traffic generated that even if all the steam locomotives had been serviceable there would have been great difficulty in them hauling all the coal trains, a total of 100,000 tons by the end of 1827. For around a decade after opening, the vast majority of passenger services were still horse drawn, there being no financial case for operating passenger trains without coal wagons being included in the formation. Such a proposal was perceived by the public to be dangerous, hence the continuation of horse-drawn passenger carriages along the route. Such a mixed traction policy was the father of mass chaos, with freight schedules being almost impossible to adhere to, confirming some of the worse fears of the proprietors.

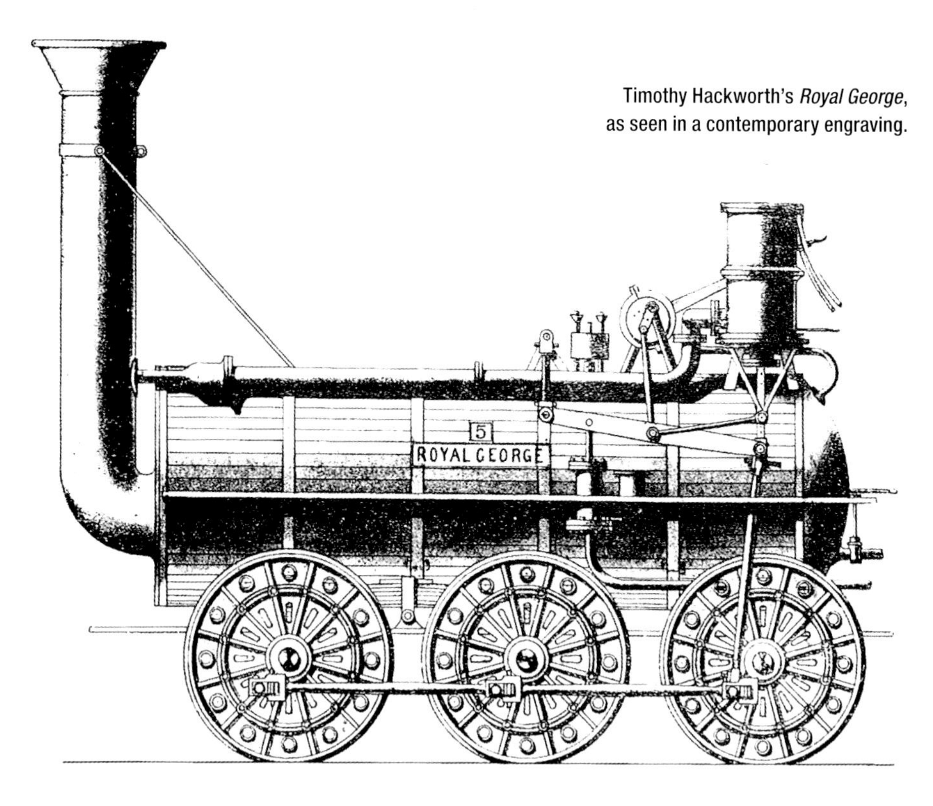

Timothy Hackworth's *Royal George*, as seen in a contemporary engraving.

RELIABLE MOTIVE POWER

It was to be late 1827 before it became patently obvious that things could not continue in this way. By this time there were four *Locomotion* class locomotives in service, and they proved to be around 30% cheaper to run than horses. However a runaway locomotive in October 1827 caused significant damage to itself and the line's infrastructure, resulting in the rapid conclusion that more locomotives were needed if things were going to improve in any meaningful way. Two new locomotives were ordered; Hackworth built *Royal George* and Robert Stephenson built *Experiment*, both being in service by early 1828. *Experiment* was an apt name for the locomotive, as it became the first such machine to have its two cylinders mounted horizontally, a stark departure from what had been, up to then, the conventional arrangement of vertical cylinders. *Royal George* was a great

Timothy Hackworth's house. RM ARCHIVE

The exterior of the Head of Steam museum in Darlington. DARLINGTON BOROUGH COUNCIL

success and revived faith in the future use of steam locomotives for use on the S&DR. So taken aback were they by its performance and capabilities, that *Royal George* became the basis for a class of six coupled goods engines that were to be the main motive power for the line for decades to come.

With reliable motive power in service, the S&DR felt confident enough to declare that all coal trains were to be locomotive hauled, with horses only to be pressed into service where there was residual traffic for them to handle. Such was the push to rid horses from the line, that the S&DR issued instructions to coal suppliers east of Brusselton that all coal had to be conveyed by locomotive-hauled trains, except in exceptional circumstances, upon which the line's management had to give permission. With some colliery owners still reluctant to use locomotives to haul their coal, the S&DR issued further instructions in 1829 stating that wagons would be held from colliery owners who failed to comply.

The operation of passenger services by six different operators created its own problems, as each attempted to outdo the other. Maintaining overall control over the sequential running of services became almost impossible, due to the fact that the line had no signalling, but passing loops at intervals of a quarter of a mile did offer some relief and allow a semblance of control, even if things did resemble organised chaos at times. Even so the order of priority was complicated and trying to enforce it became a fool's errand. Priority was given to locomotive-hauled services, with horse-drawn trains instructed to make way for them, even if it meant reversing along the track to the nearest passing loop. The biggest problem was invariably when two horse-drawn carriages, travelling in opposite directions, encountered each other on a stretch of single track. In theory a horse-drawn passenger carriage should always turn into a passing loop and await the passing of a train from the other direction before proceeding on its journey. What happened in practice, however, was rather different. It was not uncommon, indeed it was the accepted practice, for horse-drawn carriages to ignore this instruction and carry on past the loops, where they would usually meet another horse-drawn carriage head on. The typical series of events that followed usually saw first a row break out between the two stagecoach drivers, which quickly escalated into a punch-up between the two men, often followed by a mass brawl involving passengers from both carriages. Having witnessed such uncivil behaviour, Timothy Hackworth let it be known that the line's managers should go and witness such behaviour for themselves. Managers took heed and installed posts half-way between the passing points, instructing drivers that the first past the post would have precedence, with the other 'unlucky' driver having to reverse should the two meet head on. This had the unintended consequence of making drivers hurry along in an effort to be first past the post. It wasn't just horse-drawn carriages that suffered; on many an occasion horse drivers refused to use passing loops in order that a steam train could overtake, resulting in the locomotive-hauled train having to amble behind a horse-drawn train for mile after mile. Things reached a head about this time, when one horse driver, having met a locomotive-hauled train head on, refused to let it pass, despite the locomotive having passed the midway point. The managers had had enough of the various shenanigans by this point and banned the errant horse driver from the railway and summoned him before the magistrates. This was nothing compared to another horse driver versus steam locomotive incident though that resulted in a horse-drawn cart derailing, due in no small part to the driver being roaring drunk, ripping up the track as he went, before forcing another horse driver to reverse into a loop, whereupon the drunkard overturned the second horse driver's cart. Things went from bad to worse when the inebriated driver met a locomotive-hauled train and not only refused to give way but threatened to push the locomotive off the track, while waving a piece of track.

SUPERIOR RIDE

In a policy that seems utterly bizarre by today's standards, the initial concept of the S&DR was that the railway would be a permanent way, open to anyone who wished to use it upon payment of a toll, in much the same way that the horse roads had been used prior to the railway being constructed. Indeed, during the first few years of its opening, the railway was also used as a public footpath with the blessing of the proprietors. The Railway Act of 1823 set out that the public could use the line, with their horses, cattle or carriages, between 07.00 and 18.00 in the winter and between 05.00 and 22.00 in the summer months.

To avoid chaos developing, it was of paramount importance that a system of regulation was introduced and this was achieved by the proprietors ensuring that they had the monopoly on the movement of coal, for any system that enabled independent coal suppliers to access the rail network upon payment of a toll was just asking for trouble, hence why the S&DR insisted that any freight was carried in its own wagons.

It's interesting to note that the Pease family business, despite the family having substantial investment interests in the railway, was treated exactly the same as any other company that wished to move freight over the S&DR. The buying-out of the passenger services, brought about by new, reliable steam locomotives, enabled the S&DR to rid itself of the nuisance caused by horse-drawn passenger traffic. This development settled once and for all any doubts that horse power was superior to steam locomotives.

The carriages, although based on stagecoach carriages, offered passengers a far superior ride. Some of them were actual redundant horse-drawn carriages that had had their road wheels replaced by flanged rail wheels and were usually around 16ft in length.

When they were hauled by horses, the coachman had to adapt to using a brake, as the freewheeling nature of the vehicle would have injured the horses if the coachman had just pulled the animals up without a separate brake for the carriage. This brake consisted of a long lever, which connected to the wheels, operated by the coachman.

The return of passenger services being operated by the S&DR in 1833 saw horse-drawn carriages removed from the network once and for all, due to their unsuitability for such work. One of the main issues was that the shafts for harnessing horses deemed that coupling and uncoupling was an awkward and time-consuming affair.

As a result it was decided to introduce a purpose-built type of carriage that would have couplings and buffer beams. The first of these specially built carriages, which was named *Union*, entered service in November 1833 and operated between Darlington and Stockton.

Initially, there was no company livery and carriages were turned out from the works in a myriad of different colours. It was not until 1842 that the company determined that a dark red livery would become the standard colour across all its carriages. The new carriages were boxlike in appearance and consisted of three compartments, with the first class compartment being situated in the middle.

The standard of accommodation between the single first class compartment and the two second class compartments was stark to say the least. Whereas the second class passengers had to make do with hard wooden seats, those passengers travelling in first class had upholstered seats, wooden arm rests and glass windows.

One thing they had in common was the seating arrangement, where two rows of seats faced each other. No matter how austere the second class passengers no doubt considered their accommodation, spare a thought for the poor train guard that had to ride on the outside of the train, sitting on the roof, sharing the space with the luggage.

When first opened, the railway had three classes of travel, with first and second class travel being derived from the previous horse-drawn carriage practice of passengers travelling inside or outside of the carriage. Obviously, the advent of passenger rail travel saw the lot of second class passengers improve in leaps and bounds, as they also could travel inside, but third class passengers really suffered, having to travel without cover in vehicles that resembled coal wagons with seats installed. The distinction in class escalated further in around 1838, when separate trains were run between Stockton and Darlington for the use of the different classes.

One practice that developed around this time, and still continues to some degree today, is that children under a certain age could travel free. On the S&DR the age limit was under three, with children between the ages of three and 10 paying a second class fare if travelling first class and paying a third class fare if travelling second class. However, if a child travelled third class there was no reduction in fare. 'Special' fares were also introduced which, again, bear more than a passing resemblance to some of today's rail tickets in terms of the conditions attached to them, namely that they could only be used between certain times.

LNER J25 No. 1726 leaving North Rd Darlington with a Down Tebay & Barrow mineral train –20 ton wagons! December 21, 1939 JW ARMSTRONG

GREENWICH MEAN TIME

Another concept invented by the S&DR was the creation of rail heads at some of its stations, where passengers could disembark and make their way by horse and carriage to tourist destinations that had not yet been connected to the rail network. This included a horse-drawn carriage from the station at Bishop Auckland to St Helen's Auckland. By 1838, the horse and carriages had begun to be replaced by omnibuses. The discovery of numerous sulphur springs in the Darlington area helped give the fledgling tourist industry a boost. A spa was created at Dinsdale, so a connecting omnibus service commenced from the nearest station at Fighting Cocks to meet the first class trains. No such provision was made for passengers travelling at lower classes. Such was the keenness to retain and increase the numbers of first class passengers, that omnibus connecting services were soon springing up at many of the calling points along the route of the railway, conveying passengers to the tourist hotspots of the day, including the coastal resorts at Redcar, Seaton and Whitby.

Not until the introduction of Greenwich Mean Time did the rail system run to anything like its full potential. Up until then each village had its own time zone, known as 'sun time', albeit not radically different from one village to the next, depending on how far east or west it was. So rail staff had to use specially modified watches that ran fast or slow, depending on which direction they were travelling. The introduction of 'railway time' put an end to this bizarre, almost Heath Robinson type, practice, with railway times now based on London time. This policy was a forerunner to the universal use of Greenwich Mean Time. If staff were in any doubt as to the precise time, the rail company advised them to use the clock on display at the shop of clock maker Mr Harrison, which was located near the rail company's head office. If in Bishop Auckland, staff could make use of a similar facility run by a Mr Buxton and in Stockton, the town hall clock was to be used as a reference. This preoccupation with time saw clocks installed at most of the line's stations, something that was greatly appreciated by the travelling public, as only the well-off could afford watches.

LNER Darlington North Road station: the interior of the train shed, an image taken in the 1930s. *RM* ARCHIVE

Another railway practice that originated with the S&DR, and which continues to this day, was the carrying of a limited amount of luggage without payment. By 1846, the personal allowance per passenger was 100lb, increasing to 112lb for first class passengers by the following year. Passengers wishing to take their dogs by train were not so fortunate and had to pay 1s for the privilege, regardless of the distance the dog was to travel.

The personal luggage allowance increased even further for first class passengers in 1849, with an allocation of 150lb, alas second and third class passengers had to make do with 100lb.

We think of no smoking on public transport as being a relatively modern rule, but in fact, no smoking was the rule on the S&DR from at least 1840, the ban only being relaxed in 1868.

Another innovation brought about by the S&DR was the introduction of summer and winter timetables, the latter, at least initially, involving passengers having to make two changes of trains if they wished to travel the full length of the line.

The travelling conditions that third class passengers had to endure had long been a bone of contention and things came to a head in 1844, with the introduction of Gladstone's Regulation of Railways Act. This compelled rail companies to operate a minimum of one train in each direction which called at all stations and for which the fare did not exceed 1d per mile. In addition to this, the Act also required that the train travelled at an average of 12mph and that third class passengers travelled in rolling stock that could protect them from the elements. As an incentive to rail companies, these journeys were not subject to a central government tax that had been imposed on all other rail passenger journeys since 1832. This new Act gave rail passengers the kind of rights that they could never have hoped for from horse-drawn carriages; 12mph

LNER Darlington North Road Station in the 1930s. *RM* ARCHIVE

Original and replica *Sans Pareil* at Locomotion. *RM* ARCHIVE

was faster than any horse and carriage and the 1d a mile fare was cheaper too. By 1850, the fare box from third class passengers amounted to around 30% of revenue, a figure that rose to the point where it exceeded the revenue generated by first and second class passengers by 1860.

Darlington's North Road station is still in use today, served by an hourly service on the Bishop Auckland line. Prior to passenger services commencing on the S&DR, and knowing that a convenient location had to be found for a new station that was accessible to the public, it was decided to convert a goods warehouse, that dated from 1827, into North Road station, thus becoming not only the S&DR's first railway station, but the world's first railway station.

In late 1833, part of the building was converted into a shop and house, with May Simpson, who leased both, being paid the grand sum of £5 a year to keep the station clean and to ensure that the passengers were treated well. By 1842, the S&DR had taken the decision that only a purpose-built station would suffice, so the old converted warehouse was closed and a new North Road station opened a short distance to the west. This new station consisted of separate train and carriage sheds, divided by a wall, with only one through platform to begin with. A short time after the station opened, a brick-built goods depot was constructed and is now part of Darlington Railway Museum, now called Head of Steam. In September 1975, the 150th anniversary of the line opening, the Duke of Edinburgh officially opened the museum.

Shildon is now most closely associated with the National Railway Museum's outstation, known as Locomotion, but it is not as well known that it was also the village where the S&DR located its first locomotive works. The village was chosen as it was conveniently located near where steam haulage by stationary engines gave way to steam locomotives at Brusselton east incline.

When first opened it was a very cramped affair, there being just enough room to house two steam locomotives and a long shed for the fitters and other staff to work. Although it was later to develop as a place where the S&DR constructed their own locomotives, initially it was just a workshop to carry out running repairs, employing just 20 staff. The number of staff employed at the works doubled in a very short time, with locomotive construction being carried out by contractors. These included Robert Stephenson, William Kitching and William Lister and Timothy Hackworth, while he was employed by the S&DR.

TIMOTHY HACKWORTH

George Stephenson's influence regarding locomotive building was minimal, having next to nothing to do with the company once his involvement in the line's construction had finished. He went on to win many lucrative contracts, largely due to his involvement with the S&DR and the fame it had brought him. Timothy Hackworth, on the other hand, was not given the credit he deserved.

Like Stephenson, Hackworth was born in Wylam, he being born in 1786, five years after Stephenson. Both men went on to work at Tyneside collieries, with both following a path to develop the concept of the steam engine. Hackworth, following strong recommendations from George Stephenson, was appointed S&DR locomotive foreman, four months prior to the arrival of *Locomotion*. This made Timothy Hackworth the world's first shed master, another first for the S&DR! The package offered to Hackworth as an incentive was very generous. Not only did he receive an annual salary of £150, but was given a house rent free. His duties included maintaining both steam locomotives and stationary engines.

Following the unreliability issues associated with the first four *Locomotion* type engines, Hackworth was tasked with introducing locomotives that had at least the same output as these four pioneers, but with much more reliability. *Chittaprat* was bought for the low sum of £380 from locomotive builder Robert Wilson. Hackworth's main interest was in the boiler, which was found to be in good condition, following a pre-purchase exam. The name derived from the noise the locomotive supposedly made when in action. The boiler, and a number of other smaller components, went on to become utilised in the construction of Hackworth's celebrated locomotive *Royal George*. This became the first steam locomotive to have its wheels connected using outside rods. This improvement, along with its greater weight – it weighed just over 12 tons, compared to Stephenson's 'Locomotion' class of just over seven tons – gave it a significant advantage with regards to tractive adhesion, something that would prove extremely useful when moving heavy loads of coal over stiff gradients.

Locomotive crews also found much to recommend it, as it had the luxury of a footplate situated behind the boiler, as opposed to having to stand at the side. The engine proved an immediate success and so happy was the S&DR that it willingly gave Hackworth a £20 bonus for his excellent work. *Royal George* proved itself to be more successful in every way compared to the line's earlier steam locomotives, a boiler pressure of 52lb per square inch proving to be a great asset. However, it was the 141 square feet of heating surface, compared to Stephenson's miserly in comparison 60 square feet, that really gave *Royal George* its power. Within days of its introduction it was hauling trains of up to 23 loaded coal wagons and in the first two weeks it covered an average distance of 36 miles a day and it was far from uncommon to see it hauling trains of at least 46 tons.

Hackworth was ingenious by nature and his invention of the 'plug wheel' in reaction to the habitual breaking of cast iron wheels proved to be a great success. The wheel was cast in two parts – an inner and outer portion – the outer portion being secured by wedges and around 10 plugs, which linked the outer section with the inner section. A wrought iron tyre was then shrunk on to it. This ground-breaking approach not only made maintenance quicker, meaning that locomotive down time was not only greatly reduced, but cheaper too, compared to having to replace whole wheels.

Timothy Hackworth's relationship with the S&DR was far from straightforward. The S&DR allowed him, in October 1829, to enter the Rainhill Trials with his own locomotive *Sans Pareil*, which was a direct competitor to *Rocket*, designed and built by Robert and George Stephenson. Over the years there has been much controversy over whether *Rocket* was actually the best engine and that Hackworth's *Sans Pareil* only lost due to it failing during the trials, when many considered it to be the better engine. Whether *Rocket* was indeed superior we will never know, but what is certain is that Hackworth's engine went on to prove itself by being bought by the Bolton and Leigh Railway, where it went on to give many years of trouble-free running.

A change in policy by the management of the S&DR in 1833 saw Hackworth become a contractor, tasked with not only helping maintain the railway's rolling stock, but being responsible for paying its drivers too. Another change in policy came about in 1837, with the S&DR taking over responsibility for all operations on the route. Despite this change in policy, Timothy Hackworth was allowed to continue to use the S&DR's works in Shildon and, being free of the shackles of the S&DR, took full advantage of the situation by growing his own engineering business and creating his own works where he could construct locomotives for the S&DR, along with other railways.

After much searching and consideration Timothy Hackworth, rather strangely, decided to construct his new works about half a mile away from the S&DR's locomotive works. Opening in 1840, the new works was named, at a suggestion put forward by Joseph Pease, Soho Works. For many years after its opening, Soho Works was managed by Thomas Hackworth – Timothy's brother – with Timothy concerning himself with pressing S&DR matters. His contract with the Stockton & Darlington Railway came to an end in May 1840, allowing him to devote himself to developing the Soho Works as a centre of excellence in locomotive and stationary steam engine building. He also diversified into other fields, such as producing winding engines for use in collieries along with grinding mills. Sometimes the amount of work coming in meant that Hackworth had to subcontract locomotive maintenance and repair work.

The first locomotive to roll off the Soho production line destined for the S&DR was an 0-4-0 named *Dart*, which remained in service until 1879, when it finished its working life with the Great Northern Railway.

Timothy Hackworth died suddenly in July 1850, after which his son – John Wesley Hackworth – continued to run the business. He soon gave up running his father's company and in May 1853 put the business up for auction. It was bought for just under £5000 by the S&DR in July of that year. The works remained open for another 30 years, the S&DR maintaining its original nearby works at the same time.

The original *Sans Pareil* at Locomotion. RM ARCHIVE

NER 4-6-2 No. 2400 at Darlington Works, November 1922. RM ARCHIVE

DARLINGTON WORKS

Darlington Works came under the jurisdiction of many famous chief mechanical engineers over the years, including Vincent Raven, Sir Nigel Gresley, Edward Thompson and A1 designer Arthur Peppercorn.

A major employer in Darlington, it employed 3815 staff at its peak in 1954, but by the following year the British railway system's Modernisation Plan had been announced, casting a long shadow over the long-term future of the works.

Many steam and diesel locomotives had emerged from Darlington Works over the years, including A1 Pacifics, B1s, J72s and class 08s. The final steam locomotives to be built there were a batch of 10 BR Standard 2-6-2s numbered 84020-84029. This last batch of locos went to work on the Southern region, but were withdrawn for scrap just seven years later, with none making it into preservation.

Although steam loco construction had ended, new boilers continued to be made at Darlington. The last order for boilers consisted of five Gresley V2 boilers, which were completed in 1962. These also had a very short life, lasting less than four years. The first diesel to be built at Darlington was in 1952, when class 11s were built there, followed by class 08s and classes 24 and 25. The last of the diesels rolled off the production line in 1964. Numerous examples of Darlington-built diesels still survive.

Ex LNER Raven A2 Pacific No. 2402 at Darlington during the period 1923-1937. RM ARCHIVE

LNER A4 60019 undergoing overhaul at Darlington North Road Workshops on February 27, 1965. E LOWDEN (RM ARCHIVE)

LNER J39 No. 1448 around 1926 at Darlington. RM ARCHIVE

EXPANSION AND SUCCESS

The S&DR soon outgrew its two sites and following a decision in 1854, a larger site was identified near Darlington. The move from Shildon to Darlington saw the latter take on the role of a renowned place for railway engineering, with Shildon taking much more of a back seat, although it still had an important role to play in railway engineering.

The new site covered an area of 20 acres, of which only six were utilised for the new locomotive works. It opened in January 1863, just six months prior to the S&DR becoming amalgamated with the North Eastern Railway. Within a very short time of opening, the new works was referred to as the 'North Road Shops'. The opening of the new works saw 150 staff transfer from Shildon and the first locomotive to be outshopped was *Contractor*, which emerged from the works in October 1864. Although locomotives still rolled off the production line at Shildon Works, these were just assembled there, using components that had been created at North Road.

At its peak the North Road Works employed 3500 staff, making it not only Darlington's biggest employer, but also the biggest locomotive works in the country. Alas, such fortune was not to last and in April 1966 the axe fell on the works, and with it 2500 staff lost their jobs. For the final year of its operation, Darlington Works mainly concentrated on overhauling freight locomotives, closure coming on April 1, 1966, with the works being razed to the ground shortly afterwards. The majority of the site was then sold off to a supermarket chain, although the works' clock was retained to remind locals that Darlington was once the centre of the railway universe.

Contracts with third parties were terminated by the S&DR in 1853, preferring to build its own works for the maintenance and construction of carriages. The buildings, after laying derelict for many years, are now home to the A1 Steam Locomotive Trust and where 60163 *Tornado* was built, emerging from there in 2008. The trust is currently constructing No. 2007 *Prince of Wales*.

Although it would be understandable to think that the S&DR marked the start of locomotive building in Darlington, in fact this honour goes to Darlington Quaker William Kitching, who first opened an ironmonger's shop in 1790. His involvement with the S&DR started in 1824 with the supply of nails. The first locomotive to be supplied by the firm, now known as William and Alfred Kitching, was *Enterprise*, which emerged from the company's Hopetown Works in 1835, followed by *Queen* in 1837 and *Raby Castle* in 1839. By the time the company closed in 1864, it had supplied the S&DR with 16 steam locomotives, but the total number of locomotives that emerged from the works amounted to more than 200.

One of the locomotives supplied for the S&DR was *Derwent*, which entered service in 1845. Luckily this survives and is preserved at the Head of Steam museum in Darlington.

It's not hard to understand, with its numerous small forges and related industries along with skilled staff, why Darlington evolved into a major centre for locomotive builders.

William Lister also opened a locomotive works there in 1830, subsequently supplying three locomotives to the S&DR.

THE END OF CONSTRUCTION

With the ending of locomotive construction at Darlington Works, it concentrated on overhauls and scrapping instead. Darlington was well known among enthusiasts for its scrapping operations and many an enthusiast would bunk the works to wander around the scrap lines, which in 1963 included five Clan class BR Standards, 72000–72004. Strangers arriving at Darlington for overhaul included 8Fs and Jinties.

In fact the suggestion that Darlington Works be the main focal point for the

Derwent, an 0-6-0 constructed for the Stockton & Darlington Railway in 1845, is the oldest surviving Darlington-built locomotive and is also part of the Head of Steam collection. ROBIN JONES

LNER V3 No. 67629, J25 No. 65695 in Darlington scrapyard on September 29, 1962 R KELL

scrapping of withdrawn locomotives was made as early as October 1900, by the then NER locomotive superintendent Wilson Wordsall. At that time cutting up of rolling stock took place at Percy Main, Gateshead and York.

The area between Hopetown Lane and Station Road became the cutting area, but not until 1932, with Class D17/1 No. 1625, which had been withdrawn from Almouth shed on October 3, arriving in the scrap area on the 28th of that month. The majority of steam locos cut up at Darlington during these early years were of North Eastern or Hull & Barnsley origin. Three rather more glamorous locomotives did meet their end there though in 1936/37 with the arrival of the elegant-looking LNER Raven-designed Pacifics *City of York*, *City of Durham* and *City of Ripon*. Examples of the iconic large Ivatt Atlantics arrived for disposal in 1947. With the increased use of diesel traction, the number of locomotives being withdrawn soon increased, as did the number of locomotives arriving in the scrapyard. These included B16s, D49s, V3s and Q6s. This golden age of scrappings was not to last though and in

BR WD No 90378 on shed at Darlington MPD 1960s NORMAN PREEDY

the 1950s and 1960s British Rail changed its policy and began selling large quantities of withdrawn rolling stock to private scrapyards. Alas, there was no 'Barry' in the North East, so many classes became extinct. Scrapping of locomotives at Darlington Works began to wind down from 1964, with March that year seeing J94 68039 become the last locomotive to be scrapped there. During this final period, a number of locomotives were broken up in the stripping shop, where previously locomotives had been dismantled prior to overhaul.

Between 1964 and 1965 Darlington Works was home to 60103 *Flying Scotsman*, it being there for overhaul, along with A3 60052 *Prince Palatine*. To mark the completion of the overhaul of *Flying Scotsman* the works held an open day in April 1965. Also on display were *Prince Palatine*, *Tudor Minstrel* and *Blue Peter*.

It's interesting to note that at the time of closure there were 469 steam locomotives in use across the North Eastern Region and only shed staff to maintain them. Stripping withdrawn engines to keep others in service could only go so far and it soon became obvious that such methods were a fool's errand, so the decision was taken by British Rail to renew the small boiler tubes on the Q6s at Tyne Dock and Sunderland shed in an effort to keep them going until steam was eliminated in September 1967, when the number of working steam locomotives was down to a dozen.

DERAILMENTS

Within a very short time the railway's committee ordered the wagons to be modified so not only could their coal carrying capacity be increased, but for bottom boards to be installed. Robust in nature, the wagons' braking system was very basic to say the least, consisting of little more than wooden brake blocks, applied via the use of a long lever. This, however, was only a stopgap measure and it soon became apparent that a more permanent solution was required. The fixed axles continued to cause derailments, resulting in the wagons spilling their contents along the line side. Understandably, customers were in uproar. The first of the new wagons were supplied by Liverpool-based Thomas Brandreth, with Robert Stephenson and Company introducing a new spring-mounted wagon that made use of anti-friction rollers.

REVENUE

There were three main avenues from which the S&DR obtained its revenue. These could be broken down into money paid to transport freight, money paid by private operators and from the passenger fare box. It was initially envisaged, rather like rail privatisation, that private owners would be able to operate their own rolling stock along the rails owned by the S&DR, with the use being 'free' upon payment of a tonnage fee. A similar access charge was levied in the form of a toll for private operators who wanted to run their own passenger services. The third revenue stream is pretty much self-explanatory, but it's worth noting that it wasn't until 1949 that fare caps were introduced to limit the amount of money that a passenger could pay. This policy saw first class passengers pay up to 3d a mile, whereas second class passengers could pay 2d and third class 1d. Staff pay rates were drivers: 24s–30s a week, firemen 15s–18s and guards 24s–26s. As people began to realise the advantages of using rail travel rather than horse-drawn carriage, numbers rose steeply, with passenger revenue rising from £233 in the first year to £9677 by 1840. The title of station master often conjures up images of a grand position, but in the 1840s, it meant 15-hour days and helping load wagons in the sidings.

Seeing an opportunity to make money, many companies launched businesses that leased wagons to those wishing to move freight by rail. The S&DR soon got wise to this, realising that the new businesses were making considerable sums at the expense of the company. The S&DR retaliated by constructing more wagons of its own, allowing it to gain an advantage over the former. It was around this time that the S&DR realised that apportioning fees was becoming increasingly complicated due to most wagons lacking any identification as to who they belonged to. To remedy this, it instructed all owners to paint their name on wagons, along with a running number. Upon opening, the S&DR's rolling stock mainly consisted of around 150 coal wagons that had previously been used to convey coal via horse-drawn tramways. Although they had an impressive two-ton capacity they were unsuitable for the Stockton staithes due to them not being able to be unloaded straight into the hold of a ship because they were fitted with end boards, as opposed to bottom boards.

Such was the poor condition of the aforementioned wagons that the assistant resident engineer Thomas Storey informed the railway management that they were the worst set of wagons that had ever worked on a railway and, because of the poor condition of the woodwork, could not expect to remain in service beyond another two years.

60163 *Tornado* stands at North Road station, ready to work 'The Mad Hatter' charter on May 11, 2019.
GORDON EDGAR.

A quite bizarre type of wagon was introduced into service during the initial years of S&DR operation, for the conveyance of horses. This item of rolling stock, known as a dandy cart, came about as a result of problems faced by horses while hauling wagons on a descending gradient. More often than not the wagons would overtake the spooked horse, which tried desperately to catch up with the runaway wagons. The dandy cart was a low vehicle, just two feet off the ground, attached to the rear of the coal train, inside of which was water and hay for the horse. This simple, but effective, wagon allowed the horse to ride on the train during the downhill sections of route and become refreshed in between haulage duties. The horse would typically ride in the dandy cart between Shildon and Simpasture (three miles), Aycliffe to Darlington (4½ miles), from Fighting Cocks to Goosepool (two miles) and for the four miles between Urlay Nook and Stockton. Obviously, with the gradient against it, the horse could not have the luxury of hitching a ride on the return journey. The horses soon got used to the idea and would positively gallop towards and jump on the wagon at every afforded opportunity.

With the introduction of the dandy cart, the S&DR managed to increase the amount of miles per week for each horse from 174 miles to 240 miles. Some coal producers were reluctant to invest in dandy carts – at £6 each it was a considerable investment – so the company encouraged owners by stating that no help would be provided for any driver that failed to use one. To further encourage their use, the S&DR increased the price it paid for coal by an extra 1d. The last dandy cart was withdrawn from service in 1856.

RAILWAY RIVALS

It was just over a decade from the opening of the S&DR before another rail operator arrived at Darlington. The Great North Eastern Railway's plans to connect York with Newcastle were welcomed by the S&DR, for not only would it be a strategic move that would allow the proprietors to develop a network of lines in Eastern England, it would also allow the S&DR's lucrative mineral traffic to increase significantly, as the GNER route would allow its transportation over a much wider area, including into the heart of York, relatively easily and cheaply. Such was the closeness between the two rail companies that when the GNER issued its prospectus, a copy was sent to every S&DR shareholder, with the recommendation that they should also invest in the GNER if they wanted to see the S&DR continue to prosper. This intertwining of the two rail operators led to the GNER being known as the

A Stockton & Darlington boundary stone. ROBIN JONES

child of the S&DR. The first, and most difficult, section of the route to be authorised was the Newcastle to Croft section, via Darlington, authorisation being received in 1836. The next year saw the second section, linking Croft with York, authorised. Although minor work had been carried out on the northern section in the 12 months between the two authorising acts, promotor Joseph Pease turned to Robert Stephenson for engineering advice. He strongly suggested that it would be prudent to cease work on the more difficult northern section and focus all their efforts on construction of the southern section. The main reason for this was that, in light of the difficult terrain, and associated costs, that the northern section would pass through, it made financial sense to get the southern section up and running, thus bringing in much-needed revenue. This decision to abandon the northern section of the proposed route, which saw the railway sell back the land reserved for the line to its former owners, caused uproar among Durham area shareholders, who suspected that the S&DR had got cold feet over the plans and wanted to protect its Yorkshire markets for coal originating from Auckland collieries.

Construction, marked by the cutting of the first sod, officially began on November 25, 1837. In preparation for building the northern section of route first, the S&DR's Croft branch had been bought for £20,000, but was then sold back to them upon abandoning of the scheme. Right from the start the S&DR did not perceive the GNER as a threat, instead viewing it as an opportunity to be exploited, with it being granted running rights over the new line between Parkgate Junction and Croft Junction in return for ceding of the Croft branch.

The York to Darlington route opened for freight traffic in January 1841, with passenger traffic commencing two months later. This saw Darlington linked to London by rail for the first time. Initially the Darlington to York route used four S&DR locomotives for traction, two heading the southbound services and the other two double-heading on the northbound services.

Although the GNER had given up on expanding northwards, it was not the end of the line for a northerly expanding railway, for in 1842 the Newcastle and Darlington Junction Railway entered the scene with a view to taking over construction where the GNER had left it. Technically, the GNER's plans were still live, but realistically there was little or no chance of them being realised. It was with this in mind that the GNER came to an amicable arrangement with the N&DJR with regards to a leasing agreement. The news of this business deal made the S&DR proprietors incandescent with rage.

TYNE TO THE THAMES

Robert Stephenson was soon appointed as chief engineer by the new company, with the northern section opening to traffic in June 1844, although it stopped short of the centre of Newcastle, only reaching as far as Gateshead. This was of little consequence, for the arrival of the railway realised the long held ambition of George Stephenson that one day a railway line would link the Tyne with the Thames.

Although the S&DR did not think of the GNER as a threat regarding the southern section, the resurrection of the northern section by the N&DJR was a far different kettle of fish, for it allowed the S&DR's arch rival George Hudson, who was chairman of the new company, to considerably expand his reach. Such was the rivalry that the S&DR began to actively promote an alternative route north but, crucially, that was not possible by the sole use of rail. The line would only go as far as South Church, very near to Bishop Auckland, and from there passengers would have to transfer to horse-drawn carriage. This was arguably a backward step for both passengers and the S&DR.

The horses would convey passengers for around 20 miles to Rainton Meadows, the location of the Durham Junction Railway's temporary terminus. From there passengers could rejoin the rail network and catch a train to Gateshead. Unsurprisingly, people disliked this convoluted arrangement intensely and it was soon abandoned due to lack of passengers. Upon the N&DJR's route from Darlington to Newcastle opening in 1844, it soon became crystal clear that neither company could operate in a vacuum and that they would have to rub along together to some degree.

The S&DR crossing sign in Darlington: this picture was taken on December 3, 1967. R GOAD/ARPT

RIGHT: An example of original Stockton & Darlington Railway track in the Head of Steam museum. ROBIN JONES

It was to be another decade before the S&DR suffered another rail company invading its operating area, by the opening of a grand 42-arch stone-built viaduct that spanned the River Tees at Yarm, eight miles to the east. This saw the LNR encroach on to S&DR territory.

Although the height of the viaduct was considerable, it was not quite high enough to reach the top of the bank on the Durham side of the Tees. This forced the LNR to construct a tunnel beneath the Yarm Coal Depot branch before a gentle ascent to join the S&DR line near Eaglescliffe. The LNR then reached an agreement with the S&DR to cross the line at this point, but in return agreed to construct an additional two lines alongside its own as far as the junction at Mount Pleasant. These were leased to the S&DR for 1s a year, with an agreement stretching for 1000 years. Following the start of this agreement, the S&DR abandoned its main line via Preston Park. As in the case of the crossing in Darlington, trains using the new Eaglescliffe Crossing were prioritised, wth passenger trains taking priority over any other traffic.

THE CLARENCE RAILWAY

The Clarence Railway had high hopes and made no secret of its objective to tap into the lucrative market for exporting coal by numerous branches off its main line in the Durham area. With this in mind, Christopher Tennant, who was the driving force behind the Clarence Railway, promoted a shorter route for coal traffic than that proposed by the S&DR's Middlesbrough extension. At only 12 miles in length, the Clarence Railway was considerably shorter than the S&DR, but its determination to wrestle some of the coal traffic from the S&DR, which hitherto had had the monopoly on coal traffic from the south-west area of Durham, brought the two rail companies into direct conflict.

Things got very dirty between the two companies very quickly. The first obstructive act by the S&DR was to issue a ban on the use of Clarence Railway horse-drawn wagons over its railways during the hours of darkness, a period that stretched from one hour after sunset to one hour before sunrise, even though the S&DR did not abide by this. Another tactic used by the S&DR was to carry out lengthy and detailed checks on the wagons operated by its rivals. This included weighing and a detailed examination. In comparison S&DR wagons were just counted.

This attitude towards it by the S&DR appeared to make the Clarence Railway more determined than ever to succeed, and within a short time it was making a heavy impact on the finances of the S&DR.

The S&DR had one more card up its sleeve, however, and one that was to be a crushing blow to the Clarence Railway. The latter had no option but to use S&DR track to reach the pits, having no independent access of its own. This weak point allowed the S&DR to implement punitive tariffs on traffic from the mines destined to use the Clarence route. This amounted to two pence farthing the ton.

Obviously, the mine owners chose the cheaper S&DR route, creating a huge financial downturn for the Clarence Railway. It did, however, manage to cling on and even constructed a branch line, initially to Ferryhill, later extending to Byers Green, allowing it to link with the West Durham Railway. This proved very fortunate for both railways as it opened up a direct rail route between mines in the south-west of Durham to the mouth of the River Tees.

The S&DR always saw itself as being its 'own man' and not beholden to anyone, let alone another railway operator. But upon merger in 1863 the S&DR, along with its subsidiaries, had accumulated a network of 201 route miles, along with access rights to just over 54 miles.

NEW LINE

The official opening train made the journey between London and Newcastle at an average speed of 37mph. One of the most unusual features of the new route was the right-angled crossing at Albert Hill, close to North Road station, where the S&DR crossed the N&DJR. The rule book stated that, in most circumstances, passenger traffic had priority over freight traffic and that drivers were required to sound their whistle for at least half a mile prior to the crossing, continuing to do so until acknowledgement was received by the crossing signalman. There was a 10mph speed limit across the crossing and any signalman that did not report a driver breaking any of these rules was fined 5s.

Although the new line was a great achievement, the first station at the Darlington end was anything but impressive, consisting of little more than a rickety wooden shed. It is said that when Queen Victoria called there in September 1849, she did not hold back with her thoughts on the new station. Some may say it's where the "We are not amused" comment originated from!

The basic facilities did not put her off from visiting altogether though, as the queen repeated her visit for the next two years.

THROUGH THE YEARS

NER Class 1463 No. 1466 at Walkers Lane, Shildon – view east of electrification towards Simpasture Junction during the 1920s. RM ARCHIVE

LNER Q5 No. 658 at Darlington, July 20, 1938. RM ARCHIVE

NER Class 1001 No. 1275 (withdrawn in 1925 and restored to original condition for the Darlington centenary railway celebrations). DAVID R MORGAN COLLECTION (RM ARCHIVE)

LNER J21 No. 1561 leaving North Road, Darlington as V1 No 454 arrives from Newcastle, December 21, 1939. JW ARMSTRONG

Ex BR DMU awaits departure for Darlington from under the overall roof of Bishop Auckland Terminus on April 23, 1973. ANDREW MUCKLEY

NER Class A3 No. 2575 *Galopin* awaits departure at Darlington Bank Top Station in 1938. HW PONTIN (RM ARCHIVE)

BR Brush Type 2 No. 5543 loading a stone train at Frosterley Sidings on the Weardale (Bishop Auckland-Eastgate) goods line on March 7, 1973. ANDREW MUCKLEY

Ex-SR V Schools No. 30925 'Cheltenham' and ex-LMS 2P No. 40646 at Darlington Top Bank before setting off for York and Nottingham with the return RCTS 'East Midlander' on Sunday, May 13, 1962. IS CARR

LEFT: 40122 arrives at Settle with a Carlisle-Leeds service on August 17, 1983. RM ARCHIVE

BELOW: 40117 trundles through Leamington Spa with a northbound oil service in 1978. RM ARCHIVE

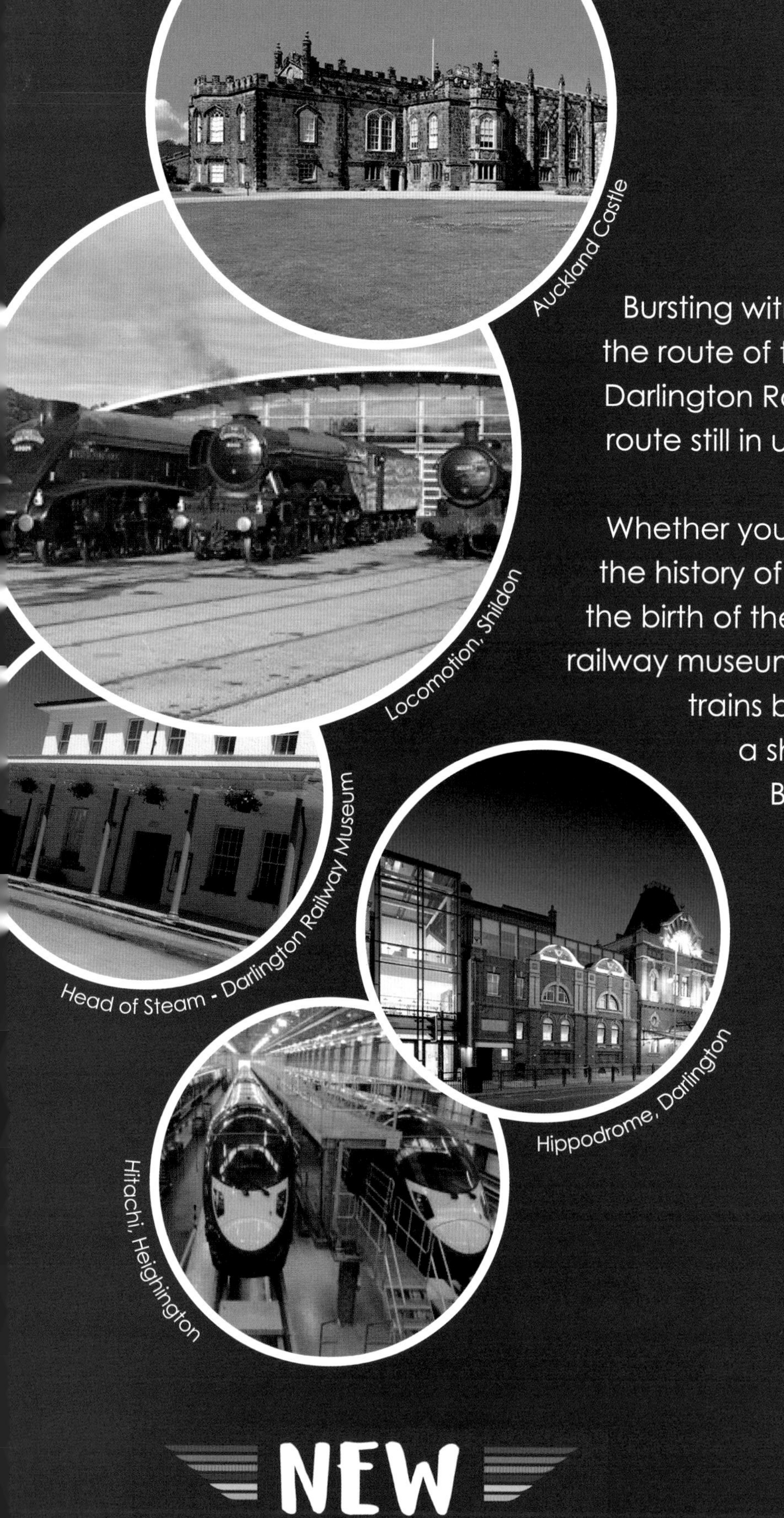

Bursting with history, The Bishop Line follows the route of the historic Stockton and Darlington Railway, the first public passenger route still in use today.

Whether you choose to immerse yourself in the history of Auckland Castle, learn about the birth of the railway at either of our two railway museums, catch a glimpse of the new trains being built at Hitachi or enjoy a show in Darlington, choose the Bishop Line to take you there.

Plus with the new hourly service it's even easier to travel on the Bishop Line.

Bishop Auckland
for The Auckland Project and Kynren

Shildon
for Locomotion

Newton Aycliffe
for Greenfield Community College

Heighington
for Hitachi, Exel Centre and UTC South Durham

North Road
for Head of Steam - Darlington Railway Museum and Skerne Bridge

Darlington
for Boutique shops, Independent coffee houses and Darlington Hippodrome

NEW TIMETABLE.

Regular trains, regular times, travel with a smile.

www.bishopline.org

A better Bishop Line, Loving our community

Chapter 2

Stations around DARLINGTON

A look at some of the most historic stations in and around Darlington.

Ask most people to name an interesting contemporary line in the UK and they will probably include the Settle & Carlisle line or the route across the West Highlands. How many will mention the Bishop Line to Bishop Auckland? Although not rich in the variety of traffic, with it just seeing an hourly DMU service, it has a rich tapestry of history going right back to the first days of the railways.

Most services to Bishop Auckland commence their journey at Saltburn, the immediate stations south of Darlington also playing a crucial part in the history of the UK's rail network.

The line between Saltburn and Bishop Auckland, which also serves Middlesbrough and Redcar, is known as the Tees Valley Line, although the section from Darlington to Bishop Auckland was rebranded the Bishop Line in recent years and is supported by the Bishop Line Community Rail Partnership. The line still survives beyond Bishop Auckland, but is not part of the national network, being operated as part of the Weardale Railway. There was regular weekday freight along the route moving coal from Wolsingham to Ratcliffe-on-Soar Power Station and Scunthorpe Steelworks, but this working ceased in 2013.

All trains along the route are currently operated by Northern with Class 142 Pacers and occasionally Class 156s. TransPennine Express operates 15 services per day in each direction from Manchester Airport to Middlesbrough via the line. Between Darlington and Middlesbrough/Saltburn there is a service running almost every half-hour during the daytime, becoming roughly hourly in the evenings. The service to Bishop Auckland is more sparse, running hourly at peak times and two-hourly off peak. A once-weekly parliamentary service in each direction stops at Teesside Airport. The new Northern Rail franchise operator Northern announced its intention to increase the service to Bishop Auckland to hourly (15 each way weekdays and 12 each way on Sundays) once the new franchise agreement came into force on April 1, 2016. The unpopular Pacer units were also to be withdrawn once new rolling stock was delivered in 2018, though the Tees Valley line will more likely see refurbished Sprinter units, rather than the brand new ones being built for Northern.

THERE ARE 12 STATIONS ON THE ROUTE:

Bishop Auckland
Shildon
Newton Aycliffe
Heighington
Darlington
Middleton St George
Eaglescliffe
Thornaby
Middlesbrough
Redcar
Marske-by-the-Sea
Saltburn-by-the-Sea

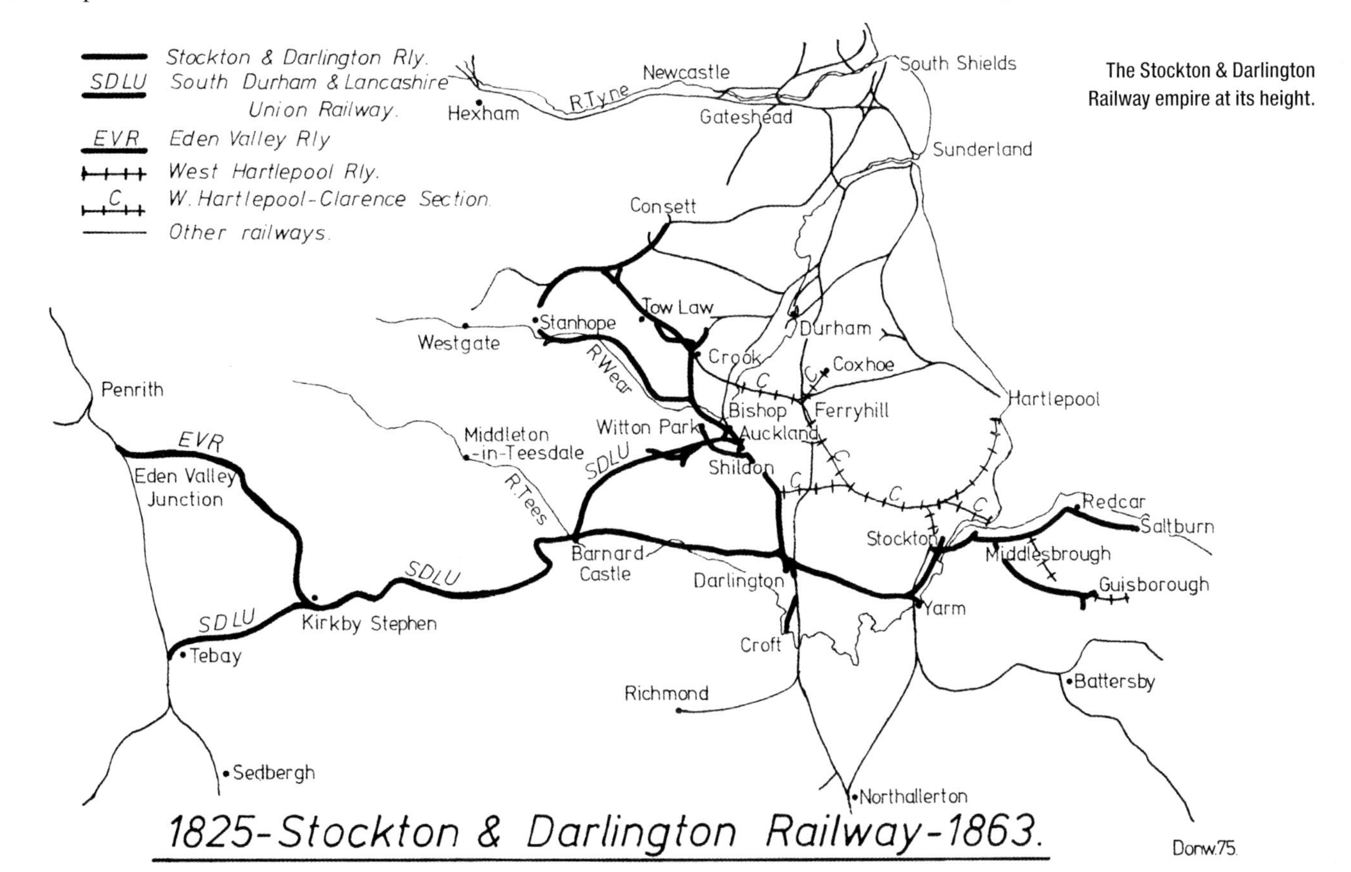

The Stockton & Darlington Railway empire at its height.

THE
MAD HATTER
60163
TORNADO

Attracting much attention from 'Darlo' locals, 60163 *Tornado* waits to depart from Darlington heading the 1Z63 08:20 North Road Darlington to Chester 'The Mad Hatter' charter on Saturday, May 11, 2019.
GORDON EDGAR

A Saltburn-Bishop Auckland service passes Shildon signalbox as it approaches the station.

But for the purpose of this publication we will concentrate on the most relevant, namely those between Middesbrough and Bishop Auckland, inclusive.

The railways reached Middlesbrough in 1830 as an extension of the Stockton and Darlington Railway. This was followed by the opening of a branch that passed just south of the new town and extended eastwards to Redcar, opened in June 1846 by the Middlesbrough and Redcar Railway Company.

Situated on the southern edge of the new town on the Redcar branch line, Middlesbrough's first passenger station was designed by John Middleton and opened on July 26, 1847. As the town expanded rapidly during the second half of the 19th century, however, the station was soon deemed inadequate to cope with the rapid growth in traffic. The station's original design made it almost impossible to expand in order to accommodate this surge in passengers, so the only option available to the railway was to demolish it, this drastic step taking place in 1874, with a new station, the one currently in use, opening in 1877.

This station was designed by the North Eastern Railway's chief architect, William Peachey, incorporating an ornate Gothic-style frontage. Beyond this an overall roof of elliptical design once existed. Constructed from wrought iron of lattice design, with glass covering the middle half and timber (inside)/slate (outside) covering the outer quarters. The two end screens were glazed with timber cladding around the outer edges. The roof was high in relation to its width.

The attractive roof was damaged beyond repair following an air raid by a German bomber during the afternoon of August 3, 1942, but lasted in situ in its damaged state until 1954, when it was removed and replaced by the current roof.

Between 2017 and 2018, the station underwent a major refurbishment to the station roof and stonework. The Wood Street car park was also upgraded at the same time and passengers benefited from the installation of new information screens as part of the scheme.

In November 2018, the Tees Valley Combined Authority approved a £20 million master plan to improve the station even further. The exciting plans include the creation of a third platform, with associated glass frontage and concourse that will look out over Bridge Street West.

This in turn will increase capacity at the station, so more trains can be introduced to serve Whitby and Newcastle, along with the reintroduction of a direct train service to London in 2021. In 2017/18, 1.313 million passengers were recorded as using the station.

Northern Rail class 156 unit No. 156464 approaches Middlesbrough station with the first service of the day from Whitby on October 20, 2012. GORDON EDGAR

NORTHERN SERVICES

All Northern services on the Tees Valley Line and Durham Coast Line call at Thornaby station, resulting in hourly services northbound to Sunderland and Newcastle and half-hourly trains westbound to Darlington and eastbound to Saltburn each weekday.

In May 2014 the timetable change saw many Durham Coast services extend through to Nunthorpe to serve the newly opened railway station at James Cook University Hospital. A number of Darlington-bound trains continue on to Bishop Auckland (running at an hourly frequency until mid-evening) and there are a pair of through trains beyond Nunthorpe to Whitby. TransPennine Express services to York, Leeds, Manchester Piccadilly and Manchester Airport also call at Thornaby every hour, with all eastbound trains calling (or terminating) at Middlesbrough.

Sundays see an hourly service along

142084 departs Heighington on June 11, 2019.
GORDON EDGAR

the Tees Valley line (two-hourly to Bishop Auckland), an hourly service to both Newcastle and Nunthorpe (with four trains to Whitby) and a two-hourly service to Manchester Airport.

Situated on the original route of the Stockton & Darlington Railway's extension to Port Darlington, Thornaby station was developed under instruction from S&DR shareholder Joseph Pease, following his sailing along the River Tees in a bid to discover a suitable site at which to locate new coal staithes downriver of Stockton. This saw 527 acres of land purchased, described at the time as a "dismal swamp" with the railway extending across the river and the creation of a station at Newport, located just north of the current Middlesbrough station.

The station and coal-handling facility was soon named Port Darlington and proved so successful that the amount of coal passing through it soon began to overwhelm the capacity available. This reached a point where the North Eastern Railway opened a new station in 1882, naming it South Stockton, opening on October 1 of that year.

Just over a decade later on November 1, 1892 Parliament granted a charter that led to the creation of the Borough of Thornaby-on-Tees, incorporating the village of Thornaby and South Stockton. This led to the station changing its name to Thornaby.

STRATEGIC LOCATION

It was an extremely important strategic location for the North Eastern Railway, which saw copious amounts of both passenger and freight traffic pass through it. It is rumoured that during the late 1890s Bowesfield Junction signalbox, situated to the west of the station and which controlled the junction where the Durham Coast lines and Northallerton/Darlington routes diverged, was the busiest box on the North Eastern Railway network.

As could be expected the main station entrance was a grand affair, with a glass covered entrance. The entrance led on to a booking office, along with a waiting room for the different classes of passengers. Of brick construction, the additional brickwork comprised creamy yellow coloured stone, which embraced the crafts movement of William Morris. A competition had been held between local stonemasons, which resulted in 104 different designs being submitted. There used to be a brass plaque commemorating the competition, but this was removed and melted down as part of the war effort during the Second World War. The platform canopies were also a work of splendour but, like Middlesbrough, suffered damage at the hands of the Luftwaffe after a bomb fell near to the station. This time, though, the damage was limited to the destruction of the glass within the canopies, not to the ironwork itself.

Following the formation of British Railways in 1948, the station received very limited repairs, but at least the staff were retained, as were the well-tended flower beds. The numerous stone carvings around the station also earned it a place in the Guinness Book of Records.

By the 1970s, passenger numbers had dwindled to such an extent that it was decided by British Rail to make Thornaby an unstaffed station. This had the inevitable result of it becoming a vandalised, unwelcoming station, leading to locals protesting at the poor state of the station and British Rail promising to refurbish it. In an act described as 'institutional vandalism' by locals, British Rail demolished the original station buildings in 1981. In 1988, and again in 1994, it was proposed that the 'bus shelter' station be renamed Stocton, a proposal that was firmly rejected. A further proposal in 2000 to rename the station South Stocton met a similar frosty reception and was abandoned following local protests.

The catalyst for the 2003 £500,000 refurbishment of the station was as a result of it being situated next to the Teesdale development area, along with Durham University's Queen's Campus. The project was led by Arriva Trains Northern and the Strategic Rail Authority, along with Stockton-on-Tees Borough Council playing a major part in the project. Upon completion, Thornaby station had regained its passenger shelters, something lacking from the station for the previous quarter of a century.

306017 awaits its turn to be restored at Locomotion on June 11, 2019. GORDON EDGAR

Officially opened by former local MP Dari Taylor on February 7, 2003, the station now has an extended car park, a heated waiting room and manned ticket office, along with passenger information displays, better lighting and enhanced security. This work saw Thornaby station win a National Station of the Year Award in 2003.

The next station along the route is Eaglescliffe. Deviating from the original course of the Stockton & Darlington Railway, this is the second station to be constructed along Yarm Road. The line had originally run to the east of Yarm Road and through Preston Hall, now known as Preston Park. It is believed that Lord Preston was extremely unhappy about the railway disturbing his livestock, so insisted that the line be diverted to the other side of the road.

GNR 251 and 'Deltic' at Locomotion.

EAGLESCLIFFE... OR EGGLESCLIFFE?

The station had originally been named Preston, having served the parishes of Preston-on-Tees and Egglescliffe. However, the railway owners were extremely displeased about having to fund the diversion of the railway, so renamed it Egglescliffe. Opening on January 25, 1853, the new line ran alongside the original Stockton & Darlington route, the latter undergoing an alignment so as to enable an easy interchange between the two routes.

The station was originally built with four platforms but by the late 1960s two had fallen into disuse and were subsequently removed.

In time, the new station became known as Eaglescliffe. The mists of time have clouded as to how the station became Eaglescliffe, as opposed to Egglescliffe, but two theories are that the written instructions to the sign writer contained the spelling error or that the sign writer presumed his instructions included an error and corrected it himself without first confirming the correct spelling.

Whatever the truth of the matter, both variations of the theory agree that the sign was not corrected for a considerable amount of time, by which time the station had become known as Eaglescliffe, as had the surrounding area.

In January 2011, construction work started on a new ticket office at the station. It has been staffed since 2012 – the ticket office is open six days per week (07:15-18:20 weekdays, 07:15-13:15 Saturdays and public holidays) and was run by an independent company (Chester-Le-Track) in partnership with train operators Northern and Grand Central and Network Rail prior to 2018.

In 2015 the station gained a heated waiting room, which replaced the previous rather basic shelters, along with toilets. Passengers also benefit from information display screens and step-free access to the platforms via a ramped footbridge.

Chester-le-Track ceased trading on March 31, 2018, resulting in the closure of the booking office. It was reopened and is now managed by Northern Rail, with staff provided by Grand Central.

Trains run twice-hourly to Middlesbrough and Saltburn eastbound and to Darlington westbound, with certain trains extended to Bishop Auckland (every two hours, increasing to hourly at peak periods). Five daily Grand Central services between Sunderland and London King's Cross also call. There is an hourly service on Sundays to Darlington and Saltburn and every two hours to Bishop Auckland.

Moving northwards, the next station is Northallerton. It was opened by the Great North of England Railway on March 30, 1841, 11 years before the Leeds Northern Railway built its Leeds to Stockton route through the town, although this did not, in the first instance, have a connection with the main line.

Rail services instead called at Northallerton Town station, located a short distance away, close to where it passed beneath the Darlington route.

The original Leeds Northern Railway route towards Melmerby was then operated as a branch line until 1901, when the NER connected it to the main line after it had constructed another junction, this time located at the southern end of the station. This then became the primary route from West Yorkshire to Teesside once again.

Meanwhile, the Wensleydale branch line to Bedale, Leyburn and Hawes had been opened in stages between 1848 and 1878. The junction with this new branch was located north of the station, with its trains making use of a bay at the northern end of the northbound island platform.

Passenger services along the branch ceased in April 1954, but the track remains in situ along much of the route for use by the Wensleydale Railway. The bay was removed in the early 1970s and there is currently no direct route to the branch from the station; due to the junction facing north, the only way trains can access the branch is via a reversing siding, accessed off the northbound main line.

The defunct south to west curve will need to be reinstated and a new platform constructed before Wensleydale trains can run to and from the station once again (the link to and from Leeming Bar was made by bus until late 2014, though a new temporary terminus has now been constructed about one mile away.

Passenger services along the Ripon line were withdrawn in March 1967 as part of the Beeching Report. The line north-eastwards towards Stockton had already lost its local passenger services by this time, but it was retained for freight traffic to and from Teesside and occasional longer distance passenger trains. It now carries a regular service to and from Middlesbrough.

Passenger numbers were 715,000 in 2017/18 and the station is staffed, with its booking office open from 05:30 each day (except Sundays, when it opens at 08:45) until 20:00. Self-service ticket machines are also available, which can be used for the collection of advance purchase/pre-paid tickets.

There are also toilets and a paper shop on the concourse, along with heated waiting rooms on both platforms. Train running information is offered via digital CIS displays, timetable posters, customer help points and automated announcements. Step-free access is available to both platforms via ramps from the subway.

The main train operator at the station is TransPennine Express. On Mondays to Saturdays there are generally two trains an hour southbound – one to Manchester Airport via York, Leeds and Manchester Piccadilly and one to Liverpool Lime Street via Leeds & Manchester Victoria. Northbound there is an hourly service to both Middlesbrough and to Newcastle.

On Sundays there is generally a two-hourly service towards Manchester Airport and Liverpool and a two-hourly service towards both Newcastle and Middlesbrough. CrossCountry services to and from Newcastle and Scotland pass through Northallerton, but do not call there.

One-time Harwich Parkeston Quay and Immingham-allocated 'B1' 4-6-0 No. 61264 arrives light engine at Darlington from Grosmont prior to taking the 1Z46 Darlington-Whitby leg forward of the 'Esk Valley' charter on Saturday, March 22, 2014. GORDON EDGAR

TEESIDE AIRPORT STATION

Teeside Airport station, with only 74 passengers making use of it in 2017/18, is one of the least used stations on the national network. This is not surprising, considering that only one train calls there every week, this being on a Sunday, and it being one mile from the airport which it is meant to serve. Originally there was a bus service between the station and the airport, but this was withdrawn some years ago. Despite 74 being a low figure for passenger use, it is significantly better than the figures for 2012/12 and 2013/14, when just eight passengers were recorded as having used the station.

Opened by British Rail on October 3, 1971, the station is on the original route of the Stockton & Darlington Railway. The station has two platforms, each of which can accommodate a four-coach train. In 2004, the airport changed its name to Durham Tees Valley Airport, but the station name was not updated. In December 2017 Durham Tees Valley Airport announced that the footbridge and eastbound platform would be closed, so as to enable the airport to save £6 million in maintenance costs up until 2022, with the once-weekly train using the remaining platform. This is a Northern operated Hartlepool to Darlington service, although other services use the line, but these pass the station without calling there.

This is all a far cry from the 1980s, when the station had an hourly service seven days a week. The 15-minute walk from the station to the airport contributed to its downfall. A 'parliamentary' service has been in operation since the early 1990s, as this avoids the need for costly and lengthy formal closure proceedings.

On October 24, 2009, the station saw its most passengers for many a year, when 26 passengers travelled to and from the station, on the only scheduled service, in a bid to raise its profile and try and persuade the railway authorities to relocate the station 500 metres nearer to the airport terminal. It has been suggested that a significant proportion of tickets sold for the station are bought by collectors, wishing to own tickets with rare destinations on them, and perhaps are not indicative of the number of people actually passing through the station.

Previously, other public transport access was frequent, with the airport being served by the 'Sky Express' bus service from Middlesbrough and Darlington. In 2011 the Middlesbrough service was withdrawn due to Stockton Borough Council's spending cuts, but services to Darlington and Hurworth remained. By 2012, passenger numbers had dropped to such an extent that all journeys to and from the airport were withdrawn.

The two-platformed Dinsdale is the last station before Darlington and can best be described as functional, with very basic passenger facilities, although these do include CCTV and waiting shelters. Passenger numbers for 2017/18 are 56,850, a slight drop on the previous period, which saw 59,110 passengers pass through the station.

Moving northwards we come to the rather basic unmanned station at Allens West, although not quite as basic as it once was, following the installation of lit waiting shelters in 2013. Passengers also have access to train running information via information screens and a long-line public address system. Step-free access is available to both platforms via the nearby level crossing.

Opened by the London and North Eastern Railway in 1940 as Allens West Halt, an unadvertised station to serve a nearby Royal Navy stores depot, it was renamed Allens West in October 1970, with passenger numbers increasing the following year thanks to new housing estates being built.

In 2013 Network Rail upgraded the level crossing from automatic half barriers to fully controlled barriers after numerous cases of pedestrians ignoring the lowered barriers, resulting in a number of near misses.

DARLINGTON STATION

Next we come to Darlington station, a station that can be described as anything but basic. Situated on the East Coast Main Line, just over 232 miles from London King's Cross, it is a Grade II listed structure. The station won the 'Large Station of the Year' award in 2005.

The first railway to use the site now home to the current station was constructed by the Stockton & Darlington Railway, with the opening of the mineral branch from Albert Hill Junction to Croft-on-Tees. This branch was subsequently purchased by the Great North of England Railway, being incorporated into its new main line from York.

The original Bank Top station structure was far removed from today's grand station and was rebuilt in the 1860s in reaction to ever-increasing traffic levels. Within just two decades, traffic levels had grown to such a degree that even this extra capacity was proving to be inadequate and causing operational problems as a result. This saw the current station created, complete with an impressive three-span overall roof, along with the construction of new sidings and goods lines. This huge project was completed in 1887.

Designed by chief engineer T E Harrison and North Eastern Railway architect William Bell, the station had a broad island platform and cost £81,000 to construct, equal to nearly £9 million in today's money. It soon became a busy interchange on the main East Coast route, thanks to its rail links to Richmond (opened in 1846), Barnard Castle and Penrith (1862/5) and the Tees Valley Line to Bishop Auckland (1842) and Saltburn (1861).

The lines to Penrith (closed in 1962), Barnard Castle (1964) and Richmond (1969) have now gone (along with the bays at the northern end of the station,

The 1M80 Shieldmuir to Willesden working at Darlington on Saturday, March 30, 2013, glimpsed passing on the station avoiding line between the tremendous Doric columns of Darlington (Bank Top) station. DB Schenker 90029 'dragged' the class 325 units throughout the diagram. GORDON EDGAR

now used for car parking), but the main line (electrified in 1991) and the Tees Valley route remain busy.

The station is fully staffed and has a waiting room and first class lounge. There is also a newsagent's and step-free access to all platforms.

PLATFORM 1:
This is the main southbound platform, with, in order of frequency, London North Eastern Railway services to York and London King's Cross, CrossCountry services to Reading and Southampton or Birmingham and Plymouth, via York and Leeds, TransPennine Express services to Manchester Piccadilly and Manchester Airport or Liverpool Lime Street, via York and Leeds, and Northern services to Saltburn via Middlesbrough, from Bishop Auckland.

PLATFORMS 2 AND 3:
These are bay platforms at the south end of the station and used exclusively by Northern services terminating at Darlington from Saltburn and Middlesbrough. Platform 2 is the platform used most frequently.

PLATFORM 4:
This is the main northbound platform, with, in order of frequency, London North Eastern Railway services to Newcastle, Edinburgh and Glasgow, CrossCountry services to Newcastle, Edinburgh and Glasgow, TransPennine Express services to Newcastle and Northern services to Bishop Auckland.

PLATFORM 4A:
This is a southern extension of platform 4 catering for trains waiting at Darlington such that they can be bypassed by trains stopping at platform 4. It is the only platform that is not under the station roof. It is used predominantly by Northern services for Bishop Auckland.

In 2017/18, 2.325 million passengers used the station.

Departing Darlington and heading towards Bishop Auckland, the first station we come to is North Road, the site of the original Darlington station. Dating from 1842, like Darlington Bank Top, it is a Grade II listed building. The 1887 opening of Bank Top station saw North Road station under threat of closure on two occasions, the first being in 1930 and the second as part of the Beeching report in 1963. Luckily it survived both attempts. However, although the station escaped closure, it did suffer rationalisation as a result of the closure of the Middleton-in-Teesdale branch in 1964.

This saw the route through the station reduced to a single track and by the early 1970s, decline had really set into the station, with the train shed not only suffering from repeated vandalism, but being deemed to be in poor repair generally. Help, was however, at hand and the awful condition of this most historic station spurred the council, along with the local tourist board and an action group led by locals, into coming to its rescue.

The result was not only restoration of the station, but the creation of a railway museum, now called Head of Steam, with the work being completed in 1975, to coincide with the 150th anniversary of the Stockton & Darlington Railway. Although the train shed roof is restored, most services do not stop beneath it, stopping instead in the open part of the platform.

The station, which saw 30,306 passengers use it in 2017/18, is unstaffed, but does have a waiting shelter, CCTV and passenger information screens. There is also a Harrington Hump installed on the platform, to assist mobility impaired passengers when boarding or alighting trains. Northern, however, does not advertise the station as being wheelchair friendly, due to the steep approach path to the platform.

Next along the route is Heighington station. Situated almost six miles from Darlington, the station boasts a delightful signalbox, dating from 1872, which controls the adjacent level crossing and the divergence of the single line from Darlington into double track. Although the signalbox remains, the semaphores were swept away and replaced by colour lights in 2014, in connection with work that saw the Hitachi plant at Newton Aycliffe connected to the national network.

The signalbox, which is Grade II listed, is one of the oldest operational boxes on the national network. Its lever frame was replaced in 1906 and extended six years later. On the opposite side of the railway line are the original station buildings dating from around 1826-27 or 1835, depending on source. The original design called for a public house which would act as a waiting room. Although the buildings no longer form part of the modern station the pub is still in use, called the Locomotion Number 1. A cobbled area outside the pub is believed to be part of the original 1825 station platform.

The unstaffed station is unusual in that it has staggered platforms either side of the level crossing. Facilities at the station were enhanced in 2013, as part of the Tees Valley Metro project. This saw new fully lit waiting shelters installed, renewed station signage, digital CIS displays and the installation of CCTV (all of the Tees Valley line stations apart from Teesside Airport and British Steel Redcar have been upgraded and provided with CIS displays).

The long-line public address system has also been renewed and upgraded with pre-recorded train announcements. Ramps leading up from the level crossing provide step-free access to both platforms.

Anybody passing through the station today may have little idea of its significance in the role of railway history, but it is without doubt one of the most historic stations in the world, although not one that many enthusiasts or tourists visit.

Situated on the route of the Stockton & Darlington Railway, it is said that on one occasion *Locomotion No. 1*'s train was rescued by navvy Robert Metcalf after he used his magnifying glass, which he normally used to light his pipe, to ignite the tinder in *Locomotion*'s firebox, after the fire went out and there was no other means of doing it. Whether that actually happened as reported is, obviously, open to conjecture. The station opened on September 27, 1825, the same day as the Stockton & Darlington Railway, and was originally know as Aycliffe Lane.

Over its history it has been renamed three times. First it became Aycliffe and Heighington, then it was renamed Aycliffe, before finally (for now!) gaining its present name of Heighington in 1874.

The station has an hourly service in each direction on weekdays; until December 2017 it was two-hourly. Passenger figures for the station in 2017/18 were 15,878.

As at a number of stations on the route, the facilities at Newton Aycliffe station have been improved as part of the Tees Valley Metro project. The enhancements include new waiting shelters and passenger information displays. In 2017/18 the station served 62,882 passengers.

The station is on the original mainline of the Stockton and Darlington Railway, where it junctioned with the Clarence Railway at what was then known as Simpasture Junction. However, the station is a relatively recent addition, having only been opened by British Rail in 1978.

DIRECT ROUTE

When the Stockton and Darlington Railway opened in 1825, linking Stockton with coal mines in the Shildon area, there was a groundswell of opinion in the town for a more direct, northerly route to Stockton, a project supported by the Tees and Weardale Railway. Two attempts to push Parliament for permission to build the line failed.

On the first occasion (1823) the plans were rejected because the standing orders had not been completed in time and on the second occasion (1824) there was opposition to the use of steam locomotives.

Although disappointed by the two rejections, the promoters of the Tees

The tremendous elegant streamlined 1930s lines of the Gresley 'A4' Pacific can be appreciated in this side-on view of three consecutive classmates. 60009 *Union of South Africa*, 60008 *Dwight D. Eisenhower* and 60010 *Dominion of Canada*, all in later BR Brunswick green livery and lined up for public viewing at the National Railway Museum Shildon exhibition centre during the afternoon of October 20, 2012. GORDON EDGAR

and Weardale railway were not to be defeated and instead proposed a new scheme to convey coal traffic to Haverton Hill, a main line that formed a junction the S&DR at Simpasture, a branch to the Deanery estate and a branch to Stockton that would provide a shorter route than the S&DR. This route didn't go into Weardale, so it was named Clarence Railway after the Duke of Clarence, later King William IV.

Following a survey of the route by, among others, Edward Steel, who was a former assistant of Stephenson, the plan gained support following a town meeting in Stockton. As part of the deal, Coxhoe Colliery was leased from the Hale sisters for a high price, with the proviso that the sisters used their influence to promote the railway.

On May 23, 1826, the Clarence Railway Act received Royal Assent, authorising a rail route of just over 26 miles between Haverton Hill and Simpasture. This included three branches; one serving the Deanery estate located near Bishop Auckland, another to Broom Hill, situated two miles north of Ferryhill, with the third branch serving Stockton. Prior to construction commencing, a second survey was carried out, which suggested that a different route be taken, one with easier gradients and fewer curves. This resulted in Samphire Batts replacing Haverton Hill as the terminus, the added bonus being that this latter choice would allow loaded ships access to the docks, even at low water.

Additional branches were planned to Sherburn via Coxhoe, Durham via Shincliffe, Byers Green and to the S&DR at West Auckland, although the latter branch was not in the bill put before Parliament. Despite stiff opposition by the Stockton and Darlington Railway along with the Marquis of Londonderry, who was building a port at Seaham and planning a railway to West Rainham, the second Clarence Railway Act received Royal Assent on June 1, 1829.

The new railway was just over 45 miles in length, with the main line to Samphire Batts now 15 miles long, the City of Durham branch was 13 miles and there were four other branches to Stockton, Deanery, Sherburn and Byers Green. After objections by celebrated English historian Robert Surtees of Mainsforth, locomotives were not allowed to traverse parts of the Byers Green and City of Durham branches.

By 1833, additional acts of Parliament enabled two more branches to be constructed and the Durham branch to be pruned at Shincliffe. Construction was far from easy, and involved the creation of a 67ft deep cutting through solid rock near Ferryhill and the creation of a 75ft embankment at Whitton of Bishopton Beck. Once the main line had been constructed between Simpasture and Samphire Batts, along with the completion of the Stockton branches , the Durham branch as far as Thrislington and the Sherburn branch as far as Quarrington, the railway desperately needed to earn some money so as to improve its cash flow.

The first coal to be carried was in August 1833, devastating the coal traffic over the Stockton and Darlington route, the latter seeing its coal volume drop from 26,000 tons to just under 9500 tons. In October 1833, the Clarence started shipping coal for export, but the S&DR continued to charge the land sale rate, rather than the lower export rate.

In January of the next year the railway had reached as far as Quarrington on the Sherburn branch and a straith was opened at Haverton Hill, with Port Clarence opening at Samphire Batts a few months later. Traffic was much lower than expected and, finding itself in financial difficulties, the company asked the Exchequer Loan Commissioners to take over management in July, and the line was managed from London.

In 1833 a branch to Chilton Pit was authorised, it opening two years later, with the Byers Green branch opening on March 31, 1837. The City of Durham branch was not built north of Ferryhill, and nor was the Deanery branch. The line was mainly double track and was originally laid with 38lb per yard rails, but later heavier ones weighing 44–45lb/yd were used. The first steam locomotive did not, however, appear on the route until 1835, horses having been used up until that point.

A colliery owner began using his locomotives after having obtained permission from Surtees, with the Clarence Railway introducing them from the following year. A passenger service was operated over the Clarence Railway between Stockton and Coxhoe from January 1836, initially by a contractor using horse-drawn coaches. In June 1838 a service using steam locomotives hauling two carriages commenced, a new contractor providing the carriages and two locomotives, Victoria and Norton. The three services a day ran the 16-and-a-quarter miles at an average speed of 18mph, the fare was 2s outside and 2s 6d inside; a horse omnibus provided a connecting service between Coxhoe and Durham.

PLANS BEFORE PARLIAMENT

In 1836, plans were put before Parliament for a South Durham railway that would connect the Clarence Railway's Byers Green branch with collieries in Weardale. The plans were rejected in 1836 and then again in the following year. In order to fulfil the legal obligation to operate a service over the Byers Green branch with a specified time period, in March 1837 a number of coal wagons were hauled by horses along the branch, as a prelude to it fully opening four years later.

Work on constructing the West Durham Railway commenced in 1837, in essence an extension of the Byers Green branch to Willington Colliery, with an Act for the line receiving Royal Assent on July 4, 1839. A two-and-a-quarter mile (3.6 km) section of line had opened on June 12, although coal was not carried until October 19, as before then locomotives were unable to be used to haul services along the Byers Green branch. From Byers Green a stationary engine was used to haul loaded wagons up a short incline, with the River Wear being crossed via a 206ft bridge, with there being two more inclines before the terminus was reached. Although the line was primarily for minerals, there was a Saturday market-day train to Stockton. This latter service was still hauled by a horse as far as Ferryhill, with a dandy cart being used by the horse after it started the train at Byers Green.

In June 1832, permission was granted for the Hartlepool Dock & Railway to construct a line connecting the coal mines in central Durham to a port in Hartlepool. This comprised of a 14-mile main line and just over nine miles of branch. The first train ran between Thornley Pit and Castle Eden in early 1835, with Hartlepool dock opening that July and the first train running between Haswell and Hartlepool in November.

In 1837 the Great North of England, Clarence & Hartlepool Junction Railway (GNEC&HJR) was granted permission for a line connecting the HD&R with the Byers Green branch, thus allowing access to Hartlepool Dock bypassing Stockton. The Stockton and Hartlepool Railway was built to keep the traffic on the Clarence by building a branch from Billingham to Hartlepool.

Construction work began in 1839, without an Act of Parliament, and the line opened to passengers in February 1841, although freight services had commenced a short time earlier. At Hartlepool an HD&R locomotive took trains forward to a 14ft inclined plane to a new Victoria Dock. The S&HR was incorporated by an Act that received Royal Assent on June 30, 1842.

Due to severe financial problems, the West Durham railway was forced to close for a number of weeks in early 1842. This had a significant impact on the revenues of the Clarence, the Exchequer Loan Commissioners taking possession of the railway that September to sell it by public auction, although the debt was settled by issuing and selling more shares. The Stockton and Hartlepool Railway leased the Clarence Railway for 21 years from September 2, 1844, and the Clarence paid its first dividend, of 1.5%, in 1845.

To prevent traffic being diverted over the shorter GNEC&HJR to Hartlepool, the WDR was linked to the Clarence Railway by 97 yards (89m) of line over private land; as this was not limited by Act it enabled the Clarence to charge whatever toll it so desired. The GNEC&HJR also found it lacked permission in its Act of 1837 to cross the Clarence to reach the Byers Green. Unable to come to an agreement it returned to Parliament in 1843, where the GNEC&HJR was able to fix a toll for traffic on the short private line and gain permission to build a bridge over the line. However, the Clarence Railway still refused to co-operate building a bridge over the line, meaning it was 1846 before the railway could be completed.

The Hartlepool West Harbour & Dock was granted permission on May 23, 1844. Port Clarence suffered as traffic was being diverted to Hartlepool and the relationship between the S&HR and the Clarence Railway soon soured. A significant number of Clarence shareholders suggested a merger with the Stockton and Darlington Railway. A permanent lease of the Clarence was negotiated, coming into force from January 1, 1851.

The Hartlepool West Harbour and Stockton and Hartlepool Railway were united from July 1, 1851. By an Act given Royal Assent on June 30, 1852, the Clarence Railway, Hartlepool West Harbour & Dock and Stockton and Hartlepool Railway were merged to become the West Hartlepool Harbour and Railway on May 17, 1853. Clarence Railway shareholders held the majority of the shares, including the much sought after voting rights.

Reaching Stockton in 1852, the Leeds Northern Railway created a junction with the Clarence Railway Stockton branch. An alliance had been formed and in anticipation the West Harbour had been enlarged from 13 to 44 acres.

From the following year the West Hartlepool moved services to the LNR Stockton station and this became known as North Stockton, the 1848 S&DR station becoming South Stockton. Hostilities soon broke out between the LNR and York, Newcastle and Berwick Railway, with the main tactic being one of undercutting each other. The 238 miles between Leeds and Newcastle dropped by 2s.

In 1862 the WHH&R found itself in financial difficulty, and in debt for over £3.7m as a result of legal action. This figure was far in excess of the permitted £2.8m. The company had purchased collieries and steam ships costing £1m, although a report the following year showed there had been good commercial reasons for buying the collieries and ships. The debt was able to be converted into shares in 1863 and a new board sold the ships at a loss, but it was not possible to sell the coal mines, as the trade in coal was depressed at the time due to the American Civil War. it was suggested that the WHH&R and NER merge, this being agreed in 1864. An Act was obtained the following year and the companies merged during the summer of 1865.

The merger of the West Durham Railway with the NER was completed in 1870, having been agreed in 1866. The NER opened a new line to Bishop Auckland in 1885 from the Byers Green branch and the passenger service was diverted over this line, this saw a new station open at Byers Green. The West Durham Railway closed west of Todhills in 1891. From 1913 former Clarence Railway lines were electrified with 1500Vdc overhead lines and electric locomotives hauled coal trains between Shildon and Erimus marshalling yard, which had opened in 1908 between Middlesbrough and Thornaby.

These trains used the former S&DR route from Shildon to Simpasture Junction, joining the former Clarence Railway line to Carlton, where a later line allowed access to the Stockton to Middlesbrough extension. The locomotives operated for two decades, until coal traffic declined to such an extent that was it uneconomical to maintain the infrastructure.

As a result of the Railways Act 1921, on January 1, 1923 the North Eastern Railway became the North Eastern area of the London and North Eastern Railway (LNER). In 1933 the rest of the former West Durham Railway was closed. In 1939 the services from Spennymoor to Bishop Auckland were withdrawn and the Billingham to Port Clarence services were pruned back to Haverton Hill. Passenger services ceased on June 14, 1954, although services for workmen continued until November 1961. In 1963 the line closed between Simpasture and the junction with the former Durham branch. The Auckland Way Railway Path follows the route of the Byers Green branch from Spennymoor, taking the route of the later NER branch to Bishop Auckland at Byers Green.

SHILDON STATION

Shildon station is one of the busiest stations on the Darlington to Bishop Auckland section of route, no doubt due to its close proximity to the National Railway Museum's outstation. Again, it has benefited from passenger information screens and CCTV, to name but two improvements, as part of the Tees Valley Metro project. Although the station itself is rather lacking in charm, Shildon does have a 42-lever signalbox, which dates from 1887 and controls a number of semaphore signals. The National Railway Museum site is built on land that was formerly occupied by railway sidings, the station having been refurbished, including the installation of a ramp in 2003 when the NRM facility was opened. Although often seen as the poor relation to the NRM's York museum, the Shildon outpost houses a large collection of locomotives and other rolling stock.

Finally, we reach the end of the line at Bishop Auckland, 12 miles from Darlington, although the preserved Weardale

37706 heads the 'Weardale' charter to Stanhope through Shildon station (with 61994 on the rear) just as the sun briefly breaks through the heavy cloud bank on October 20, 2012. GORDON EDGAR

Railway does continue on beyond the national rail station.

Bishop Trains adopted the station from Northern Rail (the train operating company at the time), providing a National Rail Ticket Office and staff for the station. Bishop Trains has further developed the ticket office and now provides a booking service for coach trips and holidays, and more recently, rail charters.

It is staffed six days per week throughout the year (Monday to Saturday 06:50-16:15). At all other times, tickets must be purchased in advance or on the train. Service running information is offered by timetable posters and Bishop Trains staff (when open). Step-free access is available from the main entrance to the ticket office and platform.

Further enhancements took place at the station in 2014. In the former toilet block, a glass front waiting room was constructed, alongside a new toilet and office. Passenger information screens have also been provided.

Chapter 3

ACCIDENTS

Darlington station has been the scene of a number of accidents over the years. Here we detail the most serious of these.

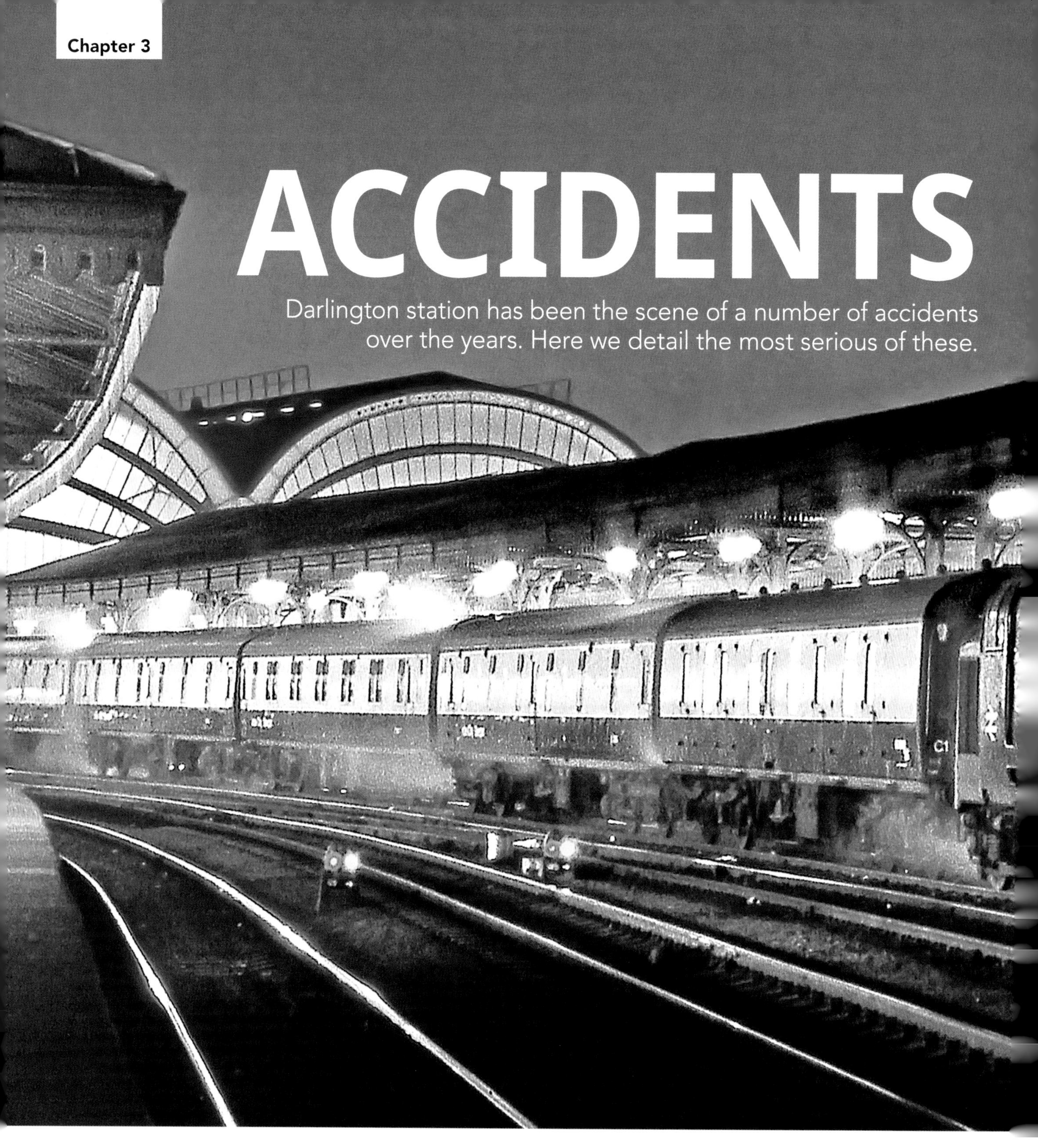

On June 27, 1928 Darlington was the scene of a serious rail accident that resulted in the death of 25 people, either at the scene, or later in hospital.

The accident involved a Scarborough to Newcastle excursion train and a parcel train shunting in the nearby sidings. The passenger train was routed on the through lines and was running under clear signals when it collided with the parcel train. The high casualty rate was as a result of the leading carriages of the excursion train, which was fully loaded, telescoping upon impact with the parcel train.

The excursion train was hauled by locomotive 2164 and comprised 11 eight-wheeled carriages. Luckily, unlike the crash at Quintinshill in 1915, the carriages, except the first class vehicle, were lit by electricity and not gas. Had it been the latter, the death toll would undoubtedly have been much higher, due to the very high risk of fire breaking out within the wreckage.

The parcel train was being shunted by locomotive 2369 and comprised 10 vehicles, including a horse box. At the time of the collision locomotive 2369 was either at a stand or had just come to a stand, the subsequent inquiry could not be certain which. What was certain, however, was that the locomotive was pushed back 185ft towards Darlington's platform 1 by the impact and suffered significant damage to its front end.

Four parcel vehicles were also destroyed by the impact, with two more suffering severe crash damage. The remaining four vehicles were relatively unscathed.

Locomotive 2164 continued for around 195ft after the collision, before overturning and mounting platform 4. The leading bogie had been ripped from the locomotive in the impact and lay near 2369. The majority of the casualties in the excursion train occurred in the rear section of the second vehicle,

55008 *The Green Howards* at York during the early hours of November 26, 1981 heading 1A45 22:55 Newcastle to London King's Cross sleeper service. The station pilot, 08525, stands in one of the up bay platforms. GORDON EDGAR

following the third vehicle overriding the underframe and demolishing the rearmost compartments.

The subsequent inquiry concluded that the blame for the collision lay with the driver of the parcel train, for he had limited experience of both shunting operations and of the signalling in the Darlington station area, leading him to pass the two signals protecting the main line at danger, and thus foul the main line on which the excursion train approached. The guard of the parcel train also came in for criticism for not acting sooner by applying the brake from his van.

Had he done so, the collision may have been avoided. No blame whatsoever was apportioned to the footplate crew of the excursion train or the signallers.

MINOR INJURIES

Another, far less serious accident occurred at Darlington station on October 3, 2009. Again, this featured two trains colliding, and again involved platform 4, but this time these were no fatalities, although a number of minor injuries were reported and two passengers were taken to hospital as a precaution.

On the day in question a London King's Cross to Edinburgh East Coast service had stopped in platform 4 to pick up passengers and while this was happening a class 142, approaching the station off the Saltburn route, failed to stop at the mid-platform signal that was protecting the East Coast express, and collided with the rear of the express train that had just started to depart the platform. As with the 1928 accident, the subsequent enquiry found that the signalling was working correctly, with the class 142 driver receiving the correct aspects on the approach to the station. The driver approached the station at 30mph, below the 35mph limit, and his application of the brakes caused the wheels to lock and the train to slide. He

BR EE Deltic No. D9020 *Nimbus* heads through Bishopton Lane Junction at Stockton-on-Tees with the 1330 Newcastle-King's Cross on November 3, 1968 – train diverted on goods lines to rear of station due to engineering work JOHN M BOYES

released the brakes before reapplying them in brake notch 2, in a bid to control the train, but to no avail and, having passed over the TPWS over speed sensor set to detect trains running in excess of 22mph, the emergency brakes were immediately applied, once again locking the wheels.

Realising that there was nothing more he could do, the driver made an announcement over the public address system, warning passengers to brace themselves for the collision.

The cause of the accident was discovered to be contamination of the rail head, probably caused by leaves, which had been crushed and carried to the southern approach of Darlington station by previous trains, from a location about two miles away. The high moisture content of the leaves would have made a significant contribution to the low level of adhesion.

The inquiry concluded by saying that a different braking technique by the driver would probably not have prevented his train from sliding past the red mid-platform signal, but could well have prevented his train from colliding with the rear of the East Coast express.

ERROR IN THE DARK

On May 16, 1872, a southbound mail train collided with a wagon which a shunter had pushed into its path at the south end of the station, where the through lines diverge from the lines that serve the station. The cause was the shunter who, with the guard, was hand pushing the wagon. He pulled the wrong ground lever and instead of the wagon taking the correct route on to the through lines, it was sent towards the Down line serving the station, where the mail train was approaching.

The two levers are within yards of each other and being dark, made it relatively easy to make such a mistake. Although a new signalbox had recently been constructed at the site, its lever frame was not yet fully commissioned and many points were still hand worked, something that was remedied within a very short time of the accident occurring.

The signaller on duty said that he could see the wagon was in a place of safety when he lowered his signal for the mail train, the wagon being pushed foul of the main line at the last moment prior to the mail train passing. Luckily, there were no fatalities, with just one lady receiving minor injuries. The inspector concluded that the main proportion of blame lay with the points not being worked from the signalbox, enabling anyone to free pull point levers, regardless of whether the signals were cleared for a conflicting move.

LNER A3 60071 *Tranquil* passes Darlington with the Up 'Flying Scotsman' on August 20, 1955. JOHN S PHILLIPS

DELTIC DRAMA

On February 16, 1977, the 08.00 King's Cross to Edinburgh service, hauled by Deltic 55008 *The Green Howards*, failed to stop at Darlington's platform 4 due to brake failure and passed the platform end signal at red, subsequently colliding with an empty stock service, formed of DMU E50213 and E56065, just north of the station.

The Deltic's footplate crew, comprising of driver A Hewitt and traction inspector J Ross, joined the train at Doncaster and between there and York the brakes responded normally, York being the last time the brakes had been applied prior to the approach to Darlington. When the driver went to make a brake application in preparation for the Darlington stop, his actions had little effect; he even stepped off the driver safety device to try and force an application, but again the Deltic did not respond. As a result 55008 sped through Darlington station at 55mph, passing signal D883 at danger before colliding with the DMU that had come off the Bishop Auckland line, overturning it in the process and the Deltic damaging its braking equipment, leading to a total loss of main air pressure.

The much heavier Deltic, now at the head of an unbraked train, continued on its way, making its way along the Bishop Auckland branch, passing another signal at danger, before coming to a stand when the passenger emergency communication equipment was operated, which had the effect of applying the brakes on the coaching stock.

Damage to the trains involved included – on the Deltic – damaged front brake and reservoir pipes, along with a buffer being torn off. The DMU suffered much more due to it overturning upon impact. Immediately after the collision it was noted that the main reservoir pipe between the Deltic and the first carriage was disconnected and the brake pipe cock on the leading end of the carriage was closed, isolating the train brakes from the locomotive. It was further noted that there had been damage sustained to the underside of 55008, which was not compatible with the collision.

Driver Hewitt had driven trains on the route for the last six years and had in fact driven the same train the day before. Speaking at the inquiry, he said that upon attempting to apply the brakes on the approach to the station the train's reduction in speed was barely noticeable, despite his brake pressure gauge for the bogies showing the correct reading, so he made two emergency brake applications, releasing the brakes after each one, which were ineffective. At that point he made a full brake application using the straight air brake and inspector Ross crossed to Hewitt's side of the cab to apply the continuous air brake. Realising the train was in trouble, driver Hewitt sounded his horn continually as 55008 sped through the platform and, after passing signal D883 at danger, braced himself for the impact with the DMU.

The aftermath of the crash,showing how 55008's nose helped cushion the impact, saving the crew from serious injury. R WILDSMITH

The DMU was not so lucky,overturning upon impact and having its bogies ripped off. R WILDSMITH

Inspector Ross confirmed that upon joining the train at Doncaster he had observed the connection between the Deltic and leading vehicle to ensure everything was in order, which it was.

During the inquiry, one very telling, but at the time of the accident deemed to be insignificant, piece of evidence came to light when steward J Campbell remarked that he and another steward had heard a banging sound from beneath their carriage as the train neared Darlington. At the time he presumed the fan belt had come off the dynamo, as the sound was very similar.

An investigation of the train discovered a traction motor cover, that had only been replaced a few days previously, missing and lodged on the leading vehicle. Upon examination, the cover was found to have numerous impact marks, which could only have been sustained by a metal-on-metal impact. The possibility of this having worked loose due to poor fitting or it being responsible for disconnecting the brake pipes and shutting the brake cock were soon dismissed as being highly unlikely. A search of the line between York and Darlington revealed nothing of any major interest, in terms of objects that the train could have struck.

Things took an unexpected turn some six months later when, on August 3, 1977 the 07.45 King's Cross-Edinburgh, hauled

by Deltic 55010 *The King's Own Scottish Borderers* struck an object between York and Darlington, which damaged and disconnected the brake pipes between numerous vehicles on the train. The train was brought to a stand, before being hauled to Darlington, where repairs were carried out in order for the train to continue northwards. Upon arrival at Newcastle it was discovered that the train heating boiler had been punctured, so the Deltic was removed from the train.

An examination of Deltic 55010 revealed strong similarities, in terms of impact marks, with the damage sustained by 55008. Again, a search was made of the tracks between York and Darlington, but this time a compelling piece of evidence was discovered near the location of the first incident with 55008, namely a piece of rail that had been split in two.

This led to the discovery of more pieces of broken rail in the grass at the side of the tracks. With this evidence, along with the damaged locomotives, the investigative team were able to piece together the probable sequence of events.

The conjecture was that shortly before the passage of both trains person or persons unknown had removed a discarded piece of rail from the cess, placed there by a permanent way gang following track repairs, and placed it across the track, being careful not to allow both ends to rest on the rail and thus activate the track circuits which would have turned the nearest signals to red. Upon striking the off-cut rail, it fractured and bounced beneath the train, causing the reported damage.

Although the footplate crew of 55008 were cleared of any blame, the guard was not so lucky. The inquiry suggested that he was not paying as much attention as he should have done. He admitted trying to calm a barking dog that was travelling in the guard van, and had he been paying more attention he would have realised that driver Hewitt was unable to control his train, and could have applied the brake in the guard van to bring the train to a halt, or at least significantly reduce its speed.

The report recommended that any surplus equipment, such as rails or cable troughing lids, be removed from the cess as soon as possible following the completion of any work, especially so where such items are of a size or weight that they can be carried by one or two people.

BOILER EXPLOSION

On April 2, 1850, the boiler of locomotive 35 exploded near Darlington station after the footplate crew had allowed the water level to drop sufficiently that the top of the firebox became dangerously hot, so that when the water pumps were activated, in preparation for departure, the water level was raised sufficiently to flow over the top. This created a huge amount of steam, due to the water coming into contact with the hot surface of the firebox, with the generated steam being too much to be released by the locomotive's safety valves, resulting in the boiler exploding.

A guard and fireman were killed as a result of a collision at Darlington station on March 9, 1929, when a Newcastle to York express collided side-on with a tank locomotive.

The express was hauled by locomotive 2205, hauling 14 carriages, equating to 311 tons, which collided with light locomotive 274 which was making its way to the shed. The impact resulted in 2205 derailing and turning on to its side, destroying the point rodding in the process, and the near destruction of the first two carriages. The rest of the train was relatively undamaged. The guard of the train – J Ringrose – and the fireman of 274 – W Carter – initially survived the crash, but succumbed to their injuries a short while later. Locomotive 274 was forced back by about 15 yards, before derailing under bridge number 99 which crossed the Up and Down main lines.

The main cause of the accident rested with the driver of 274, for not sending his

LNER A4 60025 nears Darlington with the Down Tyne Tees Pullman, July 30, 1953. JOHN S PHILLIPS

BELOW: BR Class 40 D268 restarts the 4.47pm Newcastle-Liverpool at Darlington – passing BR DMU E50622 forming the 5.40pm to Richmond on August 27 1961. RE JAMES-ROBERTSON

fireman to Darlington North signalbox to carry out rule 55, which dictates that in signalling areas with no track circuits the fireman must go to the signalbox – in this case, Darlington North was only 130 yards away – to ensure that the signaller knows that the locomotive is there. The driver of 274 insisted that he had only stood on the main line for a minute, but the inquiry concluded that it was more like five minutes.

One of the three signallers on duty at the North signalbox – one controlling the middle of the 150 lever frame and looking after the block bells, one controlling the south end of the frame and one controlling the north end of the frame – did leave the box to look along the track to see if 274 was clear of the main line, after admitting that none of them knew the precise location of the locomotive, so that the signals could be cleared for the express. The signaller saw a dim red light in the distance, and presumed 274 was still sat on the siding, but the angle of view available was far from perfect.

The report into the crash recommended that plans to install at least limited track circuits should proceed without delay.

MANSLAUGHTER TRIAL

On April 16, 1904, the double-headed 11.57 York to Newcastle passenger train collided with a light engine on the station avoiding lines between Darlington North and Darlington South signalboxes.

Although not at Darlington, the 1892 accident at Thirsk, south of Darlington on the East Coast Main Line, is worthy of a brief mention due to the tragic nature of the event and how it shone a light on bad railway management at the time.

Manor House signaller James Holmes had had only two hours' sleep in the previous 48 hours before booking on duty, due to having to care for his dying daughter. During this time he had walked many miles in a fruitless attempt to try and find a doctor. His request to management for a relief signaller to cover his booked turn was rejected and so, on the night of November 1 and 2, he briefly fell asleep, waking suddenly in a confused state, forgetting that there was a freight train standing at his home signal. In his exhaustion, signaller Holmes accepted another train into the section from Otterington signalbox, this latter train colliding with the rear of the freight. At his manslaughter trial, the judge was very sympathetic to what Holmes had been through on the domestic front and bound him over for 12 months.

The judge asked many searching questions of GNR, his employer, and it was obvious during the trial that he took a rather dim view of GNR's attitude towards a member of its staff that was obviously in dire need. Manor House signalbox has long been demolished, but Otterington remains in use as part of a private residence.

The original frame was removed upon closure, but a replacement has now been installed and passengers are able to glimpse the box as they speed along the East Coast Main Line.

Chapter 4

Looking to the EAST

In a far cry from 1825, Hitachi has made the North East its home for the building of the trains that are helping to revolutionise rail travel from Penzance to Glasgow.

60103 *Flying Scotsman* along with an Azuma, Virgin HST and Virgin DVT line up north of York.
HITACHI

The first of TransPennine Express's new Nova 1 trains left Japan on April 20, 2018 and was due to arrive in the UK two months later. Once the train completed its shipping journey, it was to begin testing across the north ahead of entering passenger service in summer 2019. The modern Japanese bullet train-inspired fleet is being built by Hitachi for Angel Trains. HITACHI

Two brand new Hitachi test trains arrived at Teesport (Middlesbrough) on March 20, 2018 after completing a two-month journey from Japan. HITACHI

Constructed between 2013 and 2015, at a cost of £82 million, the Hitachi Rail plant is located five miles north of Darlington. The site, which covers 32 acres, was just one of more than 40 sites considered by Hitachi, before opting to make Newton Aycliffe its manufacturing facility outside of Japan.

Although aware of the area's significant role in the history of Britain's railways, Hitachi's decision was primarily based on the closeness of Teesport, along with its proximity to the A1 and national rail network.

It also had enough room to enable a mile-long, electrified test track to be built parallel to the Darlington to Bishop Auckland line, allowing passengers on one of the most basic trains – a class 142 – to glimpse some of the most advanced trains undergoing dynamic testing.

Former Prime Minister David Cameron officially opened the facility on September 3, 2015. The Newton Aycliffe site includes offices, a large warehouse, along with a paint shop and 16 assembly lines, which are linked by both internal and external traversers. There is even a 23m turntable from Lloyd Somers to turn stock, so that vehicles are facing the correct way before being released from the factory. During the construction process all vehicles face the same direction, with turning only occurring once they are ready to go on the test track.

With booming order books, and hopes for many more orders to come, it was decided to invest £5 million in an additional building on the site in August 2018, which is capable of holding up to 16 vehicles. This new building, which is named Aspire, is used to house vehicles that are in need of work that can be carried out away from the production line, thus preventing any pinch points on the primary assembly lines.

The motivation to create a production facility outside of Japan was the Intercity Express Programme, which saw 866 vehicles ordered, the first one entering passenger service in 2017. This has created a boom time for the local economy, with 730 jobs created as a result. This number increased to 1300, following Hitachi winning orders to build 70 AT200 type EMUs, which included a clause in the contract with an option for 10 more, along with an order for 46x3 car class 385s (385001–385046) in March 2015 and 24x4 car class 385s (385101–385124).

The good news continued to come, with Hitachi subsequently winning orders for 356 vehicles from GWR, Hull Trains and TransPennine Express. Newton Aycliffe has become a victim of its own success so, with vehicles rolling off the production line at nine vehicles a week and little wriggle room, it was decided to construct the GWR class 802s at Hitachi's Italian plant in Pistoia, the former AnsaldoBreda works taken over by Hitachi in 2015. The booming order book at Newton Aycliffe has also seen the majority of the Hull Trains and TransPennine Express order built in Italy.

The main production hall at Newton Aycliffe is capable of holding around 60 vehicles at any one time.

Hitachi's Kasodo works is the only facility that is able to fabricate the train builder's patented aluminium body shells, using friction stir welding. The production process takes around a month to complete, with around a further month taken up by testing, and is made up of eight stages with around three-quarters of the components being sourced from suppliers within a 40-mile radius of the factory.

Not many people realise, but it was Britain that gave Japan its first rolling stock, with steam loco 150 entering service there in 1872. The small tank locomotive is now preserved in Japan.

However, prior to this Thomas Glover, who was a Scottish shipping magnate now living in Nagasaki, erected a 200-yard narrow gauge railway on the city's waterfront, described by some as a 'toy train'. Its purpose was to demonstrate the potential of railways to the ruling Tokugawa shoguns, who were very reluctant to let the Western influence into Japan.

This is set in the context of that for more than two centuries, Japan isolated itself from the rest of the world, a policy vigorously pursued by the Tokugawa Shogunate that had sidelined the Emperors.

In December 1869 the Imperial government commissioned Japan's first full-scale commercial railway, a 20-mile stretch of 3ft 6in track connecting Shimbashi Station in Tokyo with Sakuragicho Station in Yokohama. Surveying began in April 1870.

Ten steam tank locomotives, including 150, along with 58 carriages and almost 300 railwaymen, were delivered from England, and on October 14, 1872 the Emperor himself made the historic opening day trip from Tokyo to Yokohama.

An IEP on display for the opening of the Newton Aycliffe factory.
HITACHI

Work begins in Pistoia on GWR's Devon and Cornwall trains.
HITACH

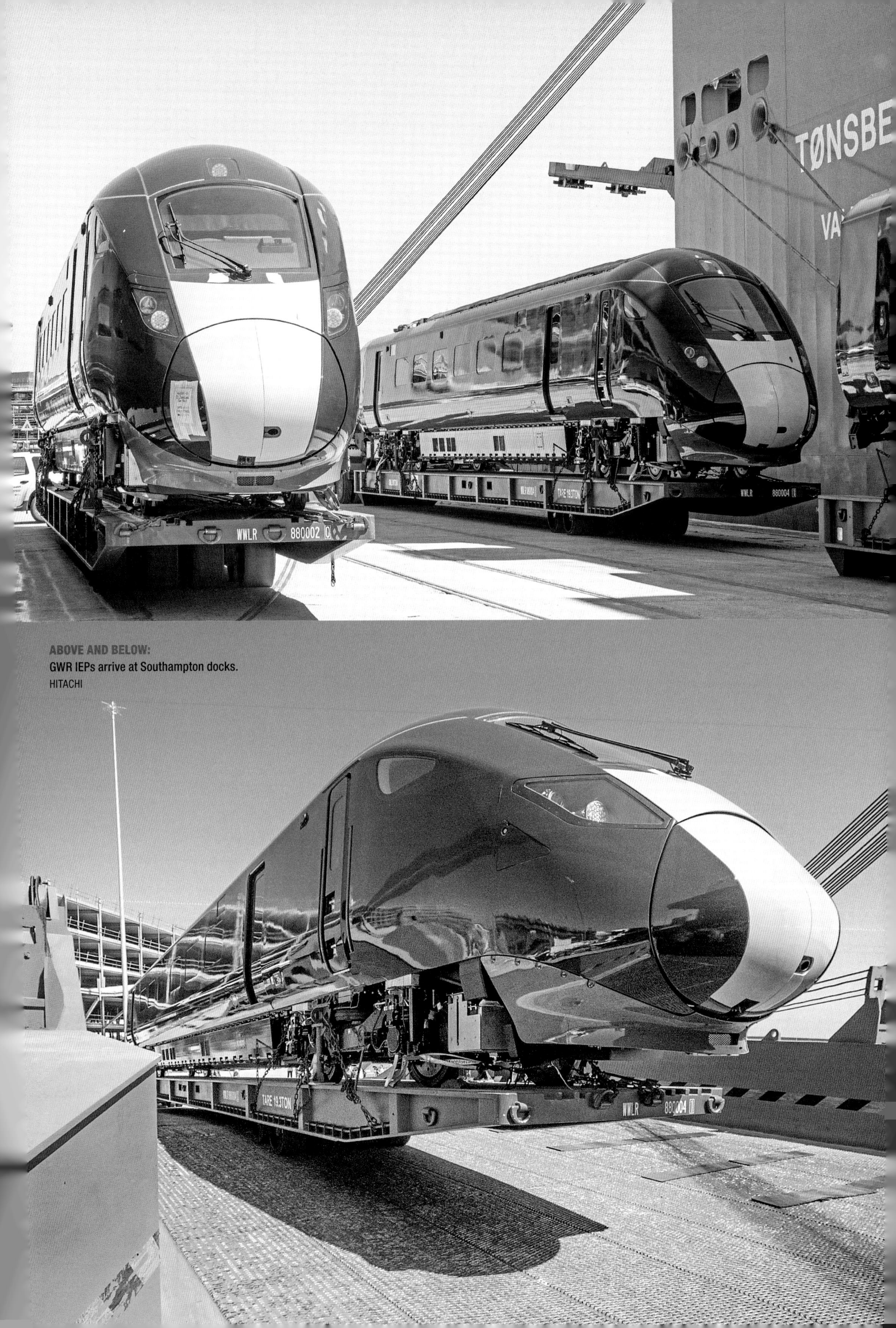

ABOVE AND BELOW:
GWR IEPs arrive at Southampton docks.
HITACHI

IEP train emerges from Newton Aycliffe.
HITACHI

Constructing an IEP at Newton Aycliffe.
HITACHI

RIGHT:
A GWR IEP at London Paddington station.
HITACHI

The first pre-series Class 800 IEP train under test at Network Rail's Rail Innovation and Development Centre.
HITACHI

RIGHT:
Japanese Prime Minister Shinzo Abe and British Prime Minister at the time, David Cameron, visited the refurbished North Pole train maintenance centre in West London.
HITACHI

New class 385s at the Newton Aycliffe factory.
HITACHI

Newly built Azumas outside of the Hitachi factory at Newton Aycliffe on June 11, 2019. GORDON EDGAR

Chapter 5

A Tornado hits DARLINGTON

Tornado has helped revive the legacy of loco building in Darlington.

The A1s were designed by Arthur H Peppercorn (January 29, 1889 – March 3, 1951), the last chief mechanical engineer of the London & North Eastern Railway (LNER). They were the last in a line of famous express passenger steam locomotives for the East Coast Main Line that included the Stirling Singles, the Ivatt Atlantics and the Gresley Pacifics.

The original 49 Peppercorn Class A1s were ordered by the LNER and built at Doncaster and Darlington for British Railways (BR) in 1948/9, after the nationalisation of the railways. As designed they were ideally suited for the postwar world of poor maintenance and heavy trains, with their 50sq ft grate allowing them to use lower grade coal than their predecessors.

The final five were even equipped with roller bearings enabling them to go for an average of 118,000 miles between heavy repairs, making the A1s the cheapest to run of all British steam locomotives in the same category. They were also the most reliable of all of the express passenger steam locomotives owned by British Railways.

Alas, the rapid onset of dieselisation in the 1960s meant that all 49 were scrapped, after an average life of only 15 years.

There was an attempt to save the last, No. 60145 *Saint Mungo*, but this unfortunately failed and it too was withdrawn in June 1966 and scrapped in September of the same year. As there was no Barry scrapyard for ex-LNER locomotives, here the story has until now ended.

60163 approaches Bedale on the Wensleydale Railway on February 15, 2019. ANDY GAPLIN

FIRST MEETING

The story to build an A1 started very humbly on March 24, 1990, when a very informal meeting was held in Darlington to discuss the possibility of building the locomotive. In April Mike Wilson, later to become the trust's first chairman, sent a letter to the railway press which culminated in the first public meeting, this being held on April 28 at the railway Institute, York.

The project team comprised of Mike, along with David Champion (a financial planning consultant who produced the marketing plan), Phil Champion (David's brother and a teacher who became the group's newsletter editor), Stuart Palmer (a Newcastle solicitor who became legal advisor) and Ian Storey (an engineer who became the project's chief mechanical engineer).

It was Ian who estimated that the cost would be £500,000, rising to £1 million, should the project take a decade to complete. This, combined with David's radical approach to fundraising, which he based around deeds of covenant, helped spur things on and make the dream become a reality.

The next step was to have a formal launch for the project and this took place on November 17, 1990 at the Railway Institute, York. It was attended by 80 people and the trust announced that the locomotive would carry the number 60163, following on from BR 60162 *Saint Johnstoun*, but the name *Tornado* had not been chosen at this early stage.

The original plan was that *Tornado* would be oil fired, but this proposal was dropped on economic grounds and instead the trust opted for conventional coal firing. The locomotive is able to carry 7.5 tons of coal and has a water capacity of 6200 gallons, with coal capacity being sacrificed in favour of water. The tender also utilises the pick-up space and has additional volume added around the top filler.

No. 60163 also has an all-welded boiler with a steel firebox and a coal grate. Unlike all other mainline steam locomotives, the engine would be air-braked throughout with vacuum brakes the secondary system. The A1 is also fitted with a sophisticated electrical system, which derives its power from a Stones turbo generator, batteries and a tender-mounted alternator. The head and tail-lights can be switched and are operated from the cab. It also has lamps for assisting in inspecting the frame and injector overflow lighting. The A1 is also unusual in having a chime whistle.

The next step was to sort and collate the original A1 drawings. Luckily many had been saved from the days when Doncaster Works overhauled the A1s. A call went out for volunteers to help sort them, resulting in Gerard Hill leading a team of six for over three days at the National Railway Museum.

In the autumn of 1991 the trust looked to start work on the tender and protracted negotiations began, with a view to purchasing *Flying Scotsman's* second tender, in order to use its frames. A ballot of covenantors revealed a small majority were in favour of a riveted (Doncaster pattern) tender, although that decision was revisited when construction moved to Darlington.

A pledge of £50,000 of sponsorship from New Cavendish Books saw owner Allan Levy select the name *Tornado* for 60163, as a tribute to the RAF crews that were engaged in the Gulf war that was being fought at the time.

By 1992 the trust had carried out detailed examinations on almost 400 documents held at the National Railway Museum, so as to determine what aspects of the original design had to be modified and updated to align with modern rail standards.

The trust had also produced a computerised catalogue of a further 300 drawings cross-referenced from those already examined.

The A1 Steam Locomotive Trust put a proposal forward to the National Railway Museum to digitally scan the original drawings to provide a compact and convenient means of storage and reproduction. This move would also allow the trust to convert the scanned drawings into vector form for modification using a computer aided design (CAD) system. The work and time put in by the research and development team, all of which had been done on a voluntary basis, was evaluated at £50,000 worth of professional time during 1992.

It was a great honour for the trust when, in 1992, former King's Cross shed master Peter Townend accepted the

A member of the footplate crew is photographed at Edinburgh Waverley as 60163 waits to depart on March 3, 2019. MANDY GRANT

60163 about to head into the night at Hansford with its demonstration freight on January 4, 2019.
MARTIN VOS

position of honorary vice-president of the A1 Steam Locomotive Trust.

Later that year, the issue of certification had to be addressed by the trust, something that is renowned for strangling even the most dedicated rail operators in red tape. Luckily for the trust, these initial fears were unfounded and they found what David Elliott called a "refreshingly flexible approach" to the trust's proposals to make design changes from Sam Foster and Brian Penney of the BR Private Owner Locomotive Engineers. Some of the major changes that the A1 Steam Locomotive Trust decided to make were, despite higher initial costs, that roller-bearings would be fitted and a number of design changes made.

These included an all-welded boiler with a steel firebox, one-piece frames, changes to the front bogie to improve the ride quality, improvements to the steam circuit, primary air (not steam) brakes and vacuum brakes, altering the balance between coal and water in the tender in favour of the latter and overall weight reduction.

With all the ground work done, it was planned to commence construction within 18 months to two years, allowing time for the original drawings to be modified to incorporate the changes outlined above. The initial optimistic date for completion was 1998, to mark the 50th anniversary of the first A1 rolling off the production line. The construction of the tender had already commenced, with the removal of the heavily corroded tender tank from *Flying Scotsman's* spare tender (tender number 5322). An examination of the frames found them to be in generally good condition, enabling grit blasting back to bare metal to go ahead, along with the manufacture of roller bearing axle boxes and horn guides.

The laborious job of cataloguing, scanning and redrawing commenced in April 1993 and at the end of several weeks (although I'm sure it felt like longer!), the small engineering team led by David Elliott had managed to unearth around 95% of the original drawings. These mostly comprised of Indian ink tracings made on linen, with just over 1000 drawings being scanned by the end of 1993.

A number of drawings contained rather ambiguous notes such as 'this bolt to be a good fit' and 'best Yorkshire Iron', which intrigued the trust engineers no end.

It was at this point that veteran railway engineer Bob Meanley joined the A1 Steam Locomotive Trust engineering team. Prior to becoming the chief engineer at the Birmingham Railway Museum, Bob had been involved in the design and construction of power stations, his engineering skills being warmly welcomed by the A1 team.

60163 rolls into Leeds with the Auld Reekie charter on March 3, 2019. MANDY GRANT

MOMENTOUS DAY

April 22 proved to be a momentous day for the trust, when the frame plates were rolled by British Steel at its Scunthorpe Works. The trust had long held the ambition to have 60163's frames cut at Doncaster Works, using the same machine that had profiled the frames for the A1s and A4s, but alas, this machine was sold just days before *Tornado's* frames were due to arrive.

Instead the new locomotive's main frames were profiled at BSD Plate and Profile Products' 38-acre site in Leeds, West Yorkshire.

Mrs Dorothy Mather, the widow of the locomotive's 1940s designer, Arthur H Peppercorn, had the honour of starting the CNC Plasma and Oxy fuel profile cutting system which cut the main frames from steel donated by British Steel. The profiling of the main frames involved cutting 25mm and 30mm plate with consistent high quality finish.

Further significant progress was made in 1995, helped by the fact that supporters and potential supporters alike could now see tangible progress being made, with the main frames being machined by TM Engineers of Kingswinford, complete with drilled holes. The frames then moved to their temporary home at the Birmingham Railway Museum.

The three-ton inside cylinder was cast in mid-June from grade 450/10 spheroidal graphite cast iron. This was followed by the casting of the left and right-hand cylinders in August. Each cylinder casting was produced from around 30 individual hand-carved patterns and core boxes, weighing more than one ton for each cylinder. The patterns were supplied on advantageous terms by Kings Heath Patterns of Cotteridge, Birmingham, the leading supplier of specialist one-off intricate patterns, with each one taking around four months to produce.

The completed castings required extensive machining before they could be fitted to 60163's frame. By this time the trust had spent around £200,000 on the cylinders, pistons, valves and various associated items.This period also saw the patterns for the six driving wheels completed, with a start being made on the front bogie and rear cartazzi wheel patterns. The casting of the six driving wheels took place at Lloyds of Burton.

The bogie side frame plates had been delivered by BSD, a subsidiary of British Steel, in late 1994 along with related items such as the buffer beam and rear rubbing plates etc. Contracts were also awarded for patterns to be made for the bottom centre and frame stays, for the bogie. These were delivered in January, being cast and machined during spring 1995.

A great bit of PR occurred in January 1995, making headlines in not just the railway press, when the RAF handed over the *Tornado* nameplates during a ceremony at Birmingham Railway Museum. Group Captain 'Raz' Ball, Station Commander, RAF Cottesmore, handed over to the trust *Tornado's* two nameplates – one with the crest of RAF Cottesmore and the other with the crest of the Tri-national Tornado Training Establishment based there – both painted by ground crews at the RAF station.

During his time at the Birmingham Railway Museum, Bob had been responsible for the design of the Bloomer replica, and had also designed the all-welded boiler for the Ffestiniog Railway's new 'double Fairlie' *David Lloyd George*. Bob agreed to be in charge of redesigning the boiler of No. 60163 to an all-welded design with a steel firebox, in order to comply with modern safety and manufacturing standards as well as to reduce costs, weight and maintenance.

Also recruited to the engineering team in 1993 were Bob Alderman, an engineering programme manager with Westland Helicopters; Steve Bell, a safety consultant with the nuclear industry; Eric Layfield, who had recently retired as power equipment engineer with Railfreight Distribution, having commenced his career as an apprentice at Doncaster Works, and Ray Pettit, who was a consultant in engineering information management systems.

The project reaching a major turning point in 1994, as it marked the year that construction of 60163 *Tornado* started. This was boosted by a major sponsorship agreement with Macreadys, the leading steel bar stockholder, part of the steels and engineering division of Glynwed International plc.

Under the agreement, Macreadys would provide The A1 Steam Locomotive Trust with a variety of steels from its wide stock range. The initial delivery took place early in the new year and comprised bright round bars for use as pins, bushes and shafts.

Another sponsor also came forward that year, namely Sheffield-based William Cook plc, the world's largest steel foundry group. Under the agreement it would make the pattern equipment, cast and machine the new steam locomotive's six 6ft 8in diameter driving wheels on very advantageous terms. All that the company asked in return was that the A1 Trust would provide it with positive publicity and approriate access. This sponsorship saved the A1 Trust a significant amount of money, as the six driving wheels would normally have cost about £60,000 to manufacture.

By this time the trust was on a roll and was able to place a £20,000 order with Birmingham-based Kings Heath Patterns, for the A1's three cylinder patterns. The objective was to have these ready over the next 12 months, in time for supporters to inspect them at the A1 Steam Locomotive Trust's convention in Doncaster, which was held in September, with the core boxes following by Christmas. The remaining two outside cylinder patterns were to follow in April and July 1995.

It was during this period that negotiations opened as to which firm would win the contract to cast the cylinders. This would take place in early 1995, with the outside two being done once the patterns had been completed. As part of the A1 Steam Trust's objective to improve on the original design of the A1s it was decided to cast the cylinders using a much higher quality steel than was used on the original batch of locomotives.

NEW OPPORTUNITIES

The breakdown in the relationship with Doncaster Council saw a great new opportunity present itself to the A1 Steam Locomotive Trust, when Darlington Borough Council offered the trust the use of the former Stockton and Darlington Railway carriage works at Hopetown, which dated from 1853. Not only was the council very supportive of the trust's aims, it helped it in applying for grant funding. The Hopetown Works became the trust's new base from 1996 and was marked with a brief ceremony involving *Locomotion*.

At this ceremony, Coun John Williams, Mayor of Darlington and leader of Darlington Borough Council, presented the key to the new locomotive works to Mrs Dorothy Mather, widow of Arthur H Peppercorn, the locomotive's original designer.

Throughout 1996, work continued apace on the locomotive's frames, with the delivery of round and hexagonal steel bars, along with frame stretchers, spring hanger brackets, bogie frame stays and firebox support brackets helping the project along. Birmingham Railway Museum staff fitted the horn blocks and horn stays, firebox support bracket (back and front), rear side rubbing plates and cross stay to the mainframes and completed the buffer beam and gussets, with TM Engineers of Kingswinford, Dudley welding the stiffeners to the bogie frame plates.

They were then returned to the Birmingham Railway Museum and awaited the delivery of the bogie frame stays and bottom centre before the assembly of the bogie could commence. Steel plate work for the cab floor was also manufactured and British Steel Engineering commenced the production process of the outside pair of cylinder castings and Lloyds had started the process to cast the rear truck and front bogie wheels.

Another milestone was reached at the Birmingham Railway Museum on May 25, with the unveiling of the three cylinders, followed by the delivery during the summer of numerous smaller, but very important, components that were necessary to complete the A1's frames. Before they could be fitted, the cylinders had to be first machined, with Ufone Engineering being given the contract. The first cylinder to be machined was the middle one, with all three due back at Tyseley in 1997. In 1996 all six driving wheels arrived at the Birmingham Railway Museum, from Burton-on-Trent-based Lloyds, prior to machining and assembly.

60163 prepares to back on to its train at Redmyre on February 15, 2019.
ANDY GAPLIN

In 1997, the news just got better and better, with the European Regional Development Fund, the National Heritage Memorial Fund and Darlington Council awarding a total of £300,000 in grants to enable the former Hopetown carriage works, which had become near derelict, to be fully restored for the A1 Steam Locomotive Trust to use as their loco building base. This not only gave the trust a dry, secure base for 60163 but also provided it with a loco pit, stores and space for machine tools. The first restoration phase of the building involved restoring the south wing, including much-needed repairs to the roof and walls, along with replacing the windows, lowering the floor and the creation of a loco pit. It was also essential that the site was made secure. Tenders were issued in late 1996, with the work being completed in late summer of the next year.

With the frames now complete at Tyseley, officially marking the existence of 60163, they were transferred to the National Railway Museum in March, 1997 on the back of an EWS wagon, thus becoming the first A1 to make its way along the East Coast Main Line in more than three decades. The move to York was only a temporary one and *Tornado* soon returned to the Birmingham Railway Museum, where its staff would continue on the frames, as per their contract.

In September, the frames departed Tyseley for the final time, arriving at the Hopetown works on the 27th, amid jubilant scenes from the gathered crowd.

Construction of the smokebox commenced in 1998, with the barrel arriving at Darlington in March of that year.

LIST OF SPONSORS

Later that year it was announced that Rolls-Royce had joined the list of sponsors; a fitting sponsor, as it was Rolls-Royce that supplied the engines to the Tornado fighters. As part of the sponsorship arrangement, Rolls-Royce machined parts of the new locomotive's three sets of motion at its Hebburn works. The motion comprised the metal rods that connected the locomotive's three cylinders to its driving wheels. The trust would have had to pay around £200,000 if it had been charged full commercial rates for this work to be carried out.

It was during this year that the plans for 60163's tender were changed. Although a limited amount of work had been carried out on the frames of the spare tender from Flying Scotsman, it was decided to sell the frames back to Flying Scotsman Services, after the latter approached the A1 Steam Locomotive Trust with a view to converting it to a water carrier for A4 *Bittern*. It was a relatively simple decision for the A1 Steam Trust, as the frames were 70 years old and in need of major modification work to make them fit for purpose. So, with this in mind, the decision was made to construct a brand new tender for Tornado.

In another big step, the 12 tyres were delivered to Ian Riley's Bury works at the East Lancashire Railway, in preparation for fitting to the A1's wheels.

A start was made on the forging of 60163's motion components in 1999. These forgings included the three connecting rods, which weighed a total of five tons and were forged into shape by the use of a one-ton air hammer. These forgings were sent in batches to Ufone Precision Engineers, based at Rowley Regis, where they were machined. By July 2000, they had been fitted to *Tornado*, having cost the A1 Steam Trust £130,000.

It's true what they say, every little really does help, and so it was with the assembly of 60163's wheelsets, the trust making a rather unusual use of Tesco's rape seed oil to enable the six driving wheels, four front bogie wheels and two trailing wheels to be fitted to their axles, by acting as a lubricant.

This method of pressing the wheels on to the axles was used to avoid damaging the roller bearings, which had to be fitted to the axles before the wheels, something that could have occurred if the more traditional method of heating the wheels and then shrink-fitting them to the axles had been used.

This trial fitting of 60163's wheels to their tyres and axles was the most complex logistical exercise carried out by the trust yet. The fitting of tyres to all 12 wheels was completed by September, although the trailing wheels had been turned to their final profile by Ian Riley, the 6ft 8in driving wheels would be more of a challenge, due to their size. The wheels were therefore taken to the Severn Valley Railway's Bridgnorth works for turning, before going back to Bury for the tyres to be fitted, before once again going back to the Severn Valley Railway for the newly fitted tyres to be turned. A £9000 order was placed with Kings Heath Patterns in Birmingham for the piston crossheads, valve spindle crosshead guides and the cylinder covers.

With completion of the smokebox shell now on the horizon, along with the smokebox door and associated fittings, thoughts rapidly turned to fitting it to the frames of 60163.

The chimney, chimney liner and blastpipe had been cast by Charles W Taylor at North Eastern Foundry, South Shields as a result of a generous sponsorship arrangement. The chimney, chimney liner, blast pipe and three steam pipes were delivered to Darlington and Ian Howitt made the distinctive superheater header covers, which are fitted to the rear of the smokebox.

These deceptively simple looking items would have been made in the past by pressing red hot plate between male and female dies. This process was not viable for making two covers, as the tooling costs would be extremely expensive. Instead, it was decided to manufacture a single male and the covers manually 'panel beaten' from 10mm plate using the former to create the right shape.

Knowing that seeing tangible progress instills confidence in supporters, and can attract new supporters, by the the time of the annual convention the smokebox and smoke deflectors had been trial fitted, the cab was in place and the loco was 'sitting' on its wheels for the first time, albeit with a large banner hanging between cab and smokebox appealing for £250,000 to fill the 'gap'.

New tyres for 60163 at the Hopetown Works on January 11, 2018. DAVID ELLIOTT

People queue to climb on to 60163's footplate at Edinburgh Waverley on March 3, 2019. MANDY GRANT

NEW CENTURY

The start of the 21st century saw the machining of the rear coupling rods completed, with machining of further rods undertaken. A start had also been made on the machining of the crosshead ready for its welding to the crosshead arms.

Meanwhile, back at Darlington, work continued apace with the fitting of manganese steel liners to the hornblocks that would allow the wheelsets to be located in the frames. An ultrasonic inspection of the axles was also carried out, to assess the integrity, an exercise that would also prove useful for creating a reference which could be compared against future scans.

Following the successful annual convention, the smokebox was removed from the frames in order that welding of the stiffening plates into the bottom of the box, fitting the blast pipe and steam pipe extensions, fitting the chimney and liner assembly and tidying up the remaining platework could be carried out.

A further grant of £10,000 from Darlington Borough Council enabled the Darlington workshop to install a five-tonne overhead crane, which proved its weight in gold, especially in tasks such as being able to take delivery of the A1's driving wheels without undue complications (and stress!). It was also used for the lifting of other large components, such as the smokebox and cab. The workshop facilities were further boosted by the kind loan of jacks from the Severn Valley Railway.

Up until now, the progress had been relatively rapid, but 2001 was to see construction work slow down and, following an approach from Darlington Borough Council, the southern section of the Hopetown Works was given over to the North Eastern Locomotive Preservation Group. This section of the works had not been required for the construction of *Tornado*, but it had been hoped that the publicity surrounding the construction of the A1 would have generated enough interest to attract other work. Alas, that proved much harder than expected. This latest development saw the machine etc. moved to the northern section of the Hopetown Works, where work continued on 60163's construction.

The year was bring more unwelcome news in the form of concerns raised over non-conformance of the new frames. This issue had been brought to the attention of the trust in 1997, shortly after their delivery to Darlington. The non-conformances were minor in nature and the £14,000 cost was borne by the contractor as part of the warranty.

While this was happening, the search continued for a manufacturer that could supply a boiler based on the original LNER design, while at the same time conforming with modern directives, relating to safety and insurance. Twelve UK firms were approached, with only three showing any interest in this prestigious contract, and even these subsequently dropped out. Thoughts then turned to Europe and Interlok, a Polish company, initially expressed an interest but gradually Dampflokwerk Meiningen emerged as the front runner. Based in the former East Germany, the ex-Deutsche Reichsbahn locomotive works was still capable of manufacturing such engineering masterpieces and, critically, was still part of German Federal Railways (Deutsche Bahn).

Things began to pick up again in 2002, with work taking place to reduce the height of 60163's cab in order to comply with the new Railtrack standard of 13 feet. Work was also marching forward towards choosing a supplier for the boiler and site visits were made to Poland and Germany to this end.

In May, the trust's vehicle acceptance body made one of its regular visits to Darlington to inspect the work as part of the certification process. By the end of the year orders for the rear steam chest covers (patterns, castings and machining) had been placed with Kings Heath Patterns at Birmingham. Production of the 'as built' frame arrangement drawing on CAD was well under way to enable detailed stress calculations to be carried out on the frame modifications (two-piece to one-piece frames) as part of the ongoing

60163 prepares to couple up to a demonstration freight at Wansford on January 4, 2019.
MARTIN VOS

60163 attracts attention at Edinburgh Waverley after arriving with the Auld Reekie charter on March 3, 2019. MANDY GRANT

certification process.

In other positive news, a new floor over the offices was on the verge of being completed, allowing the patterns to be stored in a safe and dry environment, while creating space on the ground floor for new components. In October, 60163 became a rolling chassis and this occasion marked the first movement of 60163.

MODIFICATIONS

Early 2003 saw the trust mainly preoccupied with the fitting of the Cartazzi hornblocks and hornstays. A great amount of adjustment and readjustment was required to ensure the necessary clearances were adhered to. It soon became obvious that modifications had been carried out by the LNER on the Cartazzi slides, but had not been formally recorded on any of the official drawings. As a result the trust decided to increase the nominal clearance of the axleboxes in the hornblocks from 0.025in to 0.050in.

The driving wheels, with their turned tyres now fitted, were conveyed to Darlington-based North View Engineering so that they could have their crankpins finished.

A £0.5 million bond issue was launched by the trust in 2004, to enable the boiler to be constructed and the A1 completed. Later that year, following a tremendous swell of support from the issue of bonds, it was announced that Dampflokwerk Meiningen (Steam Locomotive Works Meiningen), a workshop of the Deutsche Bahn (the German Federal Railway) and through its subsidiary DB Fahrzeuginstandhaltung GmbH (DB Rolling Stock Maintenance Company), had been chosen to construct the boiler, three years after discussions first started with UK suppliers.

With the coupling rods fitted to its six driving wheels, the A1 Steam Locomotive Trust wasted no time in announcing that 60163 was now a Pacific and also commenced work on the fitting of the remainder of the outside motion. The six cast iron valve chest liners were also cryogenically shrunk into the valve chests and the cab was returned from the North Yorkshire Moors Railway, where it had been sent for riveting.

In January 2005, the contract with Meiningen was signed, with a date of June 2006 for its completion.

A start was also made on the construction of 60163's tender, with the patterns for the hornblocks and spring guard brackets being manufactured.

Not many people know that the brake control and sanding equipment on Tornado are from two class 86 electric locomotives. Rolling stock leasing company HSBC donated the components from 86209 and 86223, with both locos being stripped at Shoeburyness. The equipment had to be overhauled though before it could be installed on the A1.

On the motion front, good progress continued to be made on the machining of the outside motion and the smoke deflector brackets had been completed, which enable the smoke deflectors to be attached to the smokebox. In addition the first of the non-ferrous fittings were finished by South Coast Steam Ltd in the form of two three-way anti-carbonisers (atomisers) which form a mist of oil and steam to lubricate the cylinders.

By early 2006, things were really moving with the A1 with the eccentric rods arriving from Ufone, for finishing elsewhere and the remaining outside motion parts being sent to Halifax-based Holts Brothers for hardening. The summer saw the last of the outside valve gear returned and the inside eccentric was fitted to the leading driving axle and the already forged inside motion parts machined.

In order to fit the injector pipe clips, the driving wheels had to be removed and piping arrived to enable the installation of the vacuum train pipe.

Following the stripping and cleaning of the class 86 sanding gear, it was discovered that only the sand traps were suitable for use on *Tornado*, with the A1 Steam Locomotive Trust volunteers adapting them to enable them to fit the A1's sand boxes, with the traps needing new air strainers. Mounting and fitting the necessary pipework was a complex situation, as the ejector layout differed from the A1 set-up.

60163
DARLINGTON

During construction of the boiler, Meiningen requested to move the mounting blocks for water gauges and blower outboard by 1.57in to allow the internal injector delivery pipes to clear the crown stays. Drawings showing the extent of the changes elicited no significant objections so authorisation was given to make the change. The safety valves were tested on A4 60009 *Union of South Africa* in May at the Severn Valley Railway prior to CE marking. This was completed by mid-June, at which point they were sent to Germany for fitting to the boiler.

The moment everyone had been waiting for finally happened in summer 2006, with the arrival in Darlington of the boiler from Germany.

There was also very good news on the tender for the A1 Steam Locomotive Trust, with a major sponsorship deal announced with William Cook Cast Products Ltd. The summer saw the tender come on in leaps and bounds, with the detailed design of the tender tank being passed to the vehicle acceptance body for approval and comments. By this stage the work on the frame was nearing completion. For financial reasons it was decided to opt for disc wheels, enabling spoked wheels to be fitted to the tender, something that at least three A1s ran with. The redesign of the tender to increase its water carrying capacity to 6000, at a slight reduction of coal carrying capacity, was also completed.

With the finish now in sight, the A1 Steam Trust had added motivation to keep the momentum going and 2007 saw many more tasks completed, including all the rods and components being weighed and the connecting and eccentric rods swung to determine the pendulum period to permit calculation of the centre of percussion and the completion of the ash pan along with its lowering into place on the frames to check the fit. In addition the wheelsets were sent for balancing at Dowding & Mills. By drilling out a pre-determined number of holes in the back of the balance weights, weight could be gradually increased until the appropriate dynamics had been achieved. Finally, the main and brake reservoir receivers were fitted to the tender frames.

In January 2008, there was still a significant number of tasks to carry out before *Tornado* could move under its own steam, but with the boiler in the frames it meant that the road to certification could start. The first tests to be carried out were the hydraulic and boiler tests, both being successful.

January 9 saw *Tornado* have a fire in its belly for the first time, it being lit by Dorothy Mather. As is the standard practice in such circumstances, the raising of pressure was a gradual process, with 100psi being obtained the following day, allowing the live steam injector to be tested. This was made possible by the assistance of the NEPLG which lent the A1 Steam Locomotive Trust the required hoses.

The official steam test was carried out on January 11, observed by John Glaze and Paul Molyneux-Berry, which proved to be successful.

After the steam test, 60163 returned to inside the works and once the boiler had cooled and been drained, construction resumed once more. The work included partially sealing the smokebox using mastic to enable the blower to function and properly attaching the chimney to the liner, setting it up in the correct position over the blast pipes and bolting it to the smokebox.

On February 6, the tender tank was delivered to Darlington from North View Engineering and trial fitted to the frames. This exercise proved successful and it was removed, being placed on wooden blocks while work continued on the plumbing and electrical side. The summer saw drawings for the banjo dome sent to the North Norfolk Railway, so they could manufacture it and on July 3, 2008, *Tornado* was placed on her springs for the first time, exactly 70 years to within an hour since A4 4468 *Mallard* reached the world steam speed record of 126mph. The remainder of July was occupied with the fitting of electrical cable and wiring up the components in the cubicles, finishing the cab fittings, completing the air braking systems and preparing and painting the loco and tender in works grey, this latter job being undertaken by Ian Matthews to an extremely high standard.

The next month saw *Tornado* move under its own steam for the first time, albeit only a short distance within the yard of the Hopetown Works. Dorothy Mather even had a ride on the footplate.

The next step was to find somewhere where 60163 could undergo running-in trials. The Great Central Railway readily agreed to this, which meant that the A1 Steam Locomotive Trust could take advantage of the line's capability to run test trains at 60mph. It was during its stay in Leicestershire that the A1 hauled its first public passenger trains.

A move to the National Railway Museum followed in November, which became 60163's mainline base for its three test runs, the final one of the three being a 75mph return run to Newcastle.

Tornado then entered the paint shop at the National Railway Museum, before emerging in LNER apple green the next month, in front of a huge welcoming crowd.

LEFT: 60163 on a charter freight at the Nene Valley Railway on January 4, 2019. MARTIN VOS

Chapter 6

BY ROYAL Appointment

Spurred on by the success of *Tornado*, work on P2 2007 *Prince of Wales* is advancing at an incredible rate.

After a time, A1 Steam Locomotive Trust members turned their thoughts to what they could build next. After a period of deliberation it was decided in 2010, after a feasibility study, to construct a Gresley P2, none of which survived into preservation. The P2 was a small class of just six locomotives, numbered 2001-2006, built to eliminate the use of double-headers on the heavy Edinburgh to Aberdeen sleeper services.

The first of the class – 2001 *Cock O' The North* – emerged from the hallowed Doncaster Works in 1934, becoming Britain's most powerful passenger steam locomotive. Although 2001 and 2002 *Earl Marischal* rolled off the production line with a rather rudimentary style of streamlining, 2003 *Lord President* and the other three members carried full streamlining, not dissimilar to that used on the A4s. However, 2001 and 2002 were subsequently rebuilt to present a uniform appearance across the class. There were a few minor differences among the individual class members and these included 2004 *Mons Meg* having a bypass valve installed to reduce the draw in the fire from the exhaust, with 2005 *Thane of Fife* having a single chimney fitted and 2006 *Wolf of Badenoch* using a diagram 108 boiler, to assist with combustion.

The pictures show 2007 being rolled out of the Hopetown works in June 2018. DAVID ELLIOTT

Although they put in an impressive performance, the death of Sir Nigel Gresley in 1941, coupled with the Ssecond World War, hampered further development of the P2s. It was believed that in time, the teething problems such as failure of crank axles, along with the design faults inherent in the swing link pony truck suspension that led to a number of derailments on sharp curves within depots, could have been cured.

Gresley's successor Thompson did not persevere with finding a cure and instead took the option of rebuilding the 2-8-2 P2s as 4-6-2 A2/2s, with 2005 being the first to emerge from Doncaster works in January 1943. According to Thompson the rebuilt locomotives were significantly more reliable, yet, again according to Thompson, still retained

DAVID ELLIOTT

their ability to haul the heavy loads for which the P2s were designed. It transpired, however, that Thompson was being rather optimistic and that the rebuilt locomotives were nowhere near as reliable as he led others to believe. The same went for their haulage capability, which had been reduced. This signalled the end for the class and in November 1959, 60505 *Thane of Fife* became the first of the former LNER pacifics to be withdrawn, its last shed being New England. Next to go was York allocated 60503 *Lord President*, also in November. Both ended up being cut up at Doncaster Works within weeks of each other. The others were not far behind; all were gone by June 1961.

Following the positive outcome of the feasibility study by Delta Rail to build an improved Gresley P2, the project was formally launched at the trust's 2013 convention and a subsidiary company – The P2 Steam Locomotive Company – was formed.

As with *Tornado*, *Prince of Wales* will not be a precise replica, hence it being allocated the number 2007 – the next sequential P2 number – and it will be initially launched in LNER apple green. The new locomotive will, just as 60163 was, undergo a number of modifications to improve its performance compared to the LNER-built examples. It will, however, be visually almost identical.

One of the main modifications is, not surprisingly, to the troublesome pony truck, the original swing link design being replaced with a spring side design, very similar to those fitted to the V2s. The crank axle has also undergone a redesign to avoid any potential failures, a feature of the original P2s, with the class suffering around four such failures while in traffic. It was only through luck that these incidents occurred during low speed movements, thus avoiding any derailments. It is thought that the failures were as a result of the P2s and A3s sharing the same crank axle design,

MANDY GRANT

MANDY GRANT

MANDY GRANT

DAVID ELLIOTT

but crucially the increased cylinder size of the P2s exerted greater torque on the axles and where this could have been dissipated on the A3s via wheel slip, the P2s were much more sure-footed, meaning that the force had no way to escape except via the axle.

Turning to the frames, these incorporate many of *Tornado's* features, such as roller bearings and alterations to the frame stays in order to accommodate the air-braking equipment. There has also been a redesign of the cylinder block, compared to that on the LNER P2s, in an effort to improve efficiency by reducing consumption of coal and water.

The boiler on 2007 is of the same dimensions as that used on *Tornado*, although the original P2s had a boiler that was 17 inches longer. This minor difference will pass unnoticed by most people, the public and enthusiast alike, but to help disguise this minor difference in length, a slightly longer smokebox has been fitted. The upside to this modification is that it is likely that a longer smokebox will reduce the possibility of the fire being pulled apart by the P2's sharp exhaust.

Lentz-designed rotary valve gear, as was fitted on *Cock O' The North*, will be installed on 2007, although excessive wear and tear on the cams and followers was a marked downside to this equipment, the plus side being that it enabled the driver to choose an almost infinite number of cut-off settings in order to get the most efficient use out of the loco.

The P2 group briefly considered using a Caprotti valve gear, as used on 71000 *Duke of Gloucester* but this was dismissed in favour of a US-developed Franklin valve gear, which is a derivative of the Lentz design. As with *Tornado* the P2 tender will be modified to obtain the ideal coal/water ratio; the P2 will also make use of a similar electrical system to that used on 60163.

FUNDING DIFFERENCES

One major difference between the building of the A1 and P2 is in the way of funding. Whereas *Tornado's* construction was partially funded via loans, it is intended that the construction of *Prince of Wales* will be debt-free upon its completion. This has resulted in a rather different approach to fundraising, with a number of clubs being created – such as The Founders Club – which set itself an objective of 100 supporters raising a total of £100,000, which would provide the finance for the cutting of the frames. This proved a winning formula and within just four months more than 250 supporters had joined the club, with the frame plates being produced from Scunthorpe steel works in April 2014 and arriving at the Hopetown Works three months later, with construction taking place a few weeks later.

The success of The Founders Club spurred on the P2 group to create other clubs that will fund the boiler and other large components. To date just over £3 million has either been raised or pledged towards the £5 million required to complete the P2, with an estimated completion date of 2021.

As was the case with *Tornado*, progress on *Prince of Wales* is continuing at a rapid pace, with the frames already housing the cab, running plate and smokebox.

The now-removed boiler cladding, held in place by a jig, gave a realistic idea of how the P2 will look once the boiler is lifted into the frames. For a short while the P2 became a rolling chassis when the driving wheels were installed during August 2018 as a trial fit.

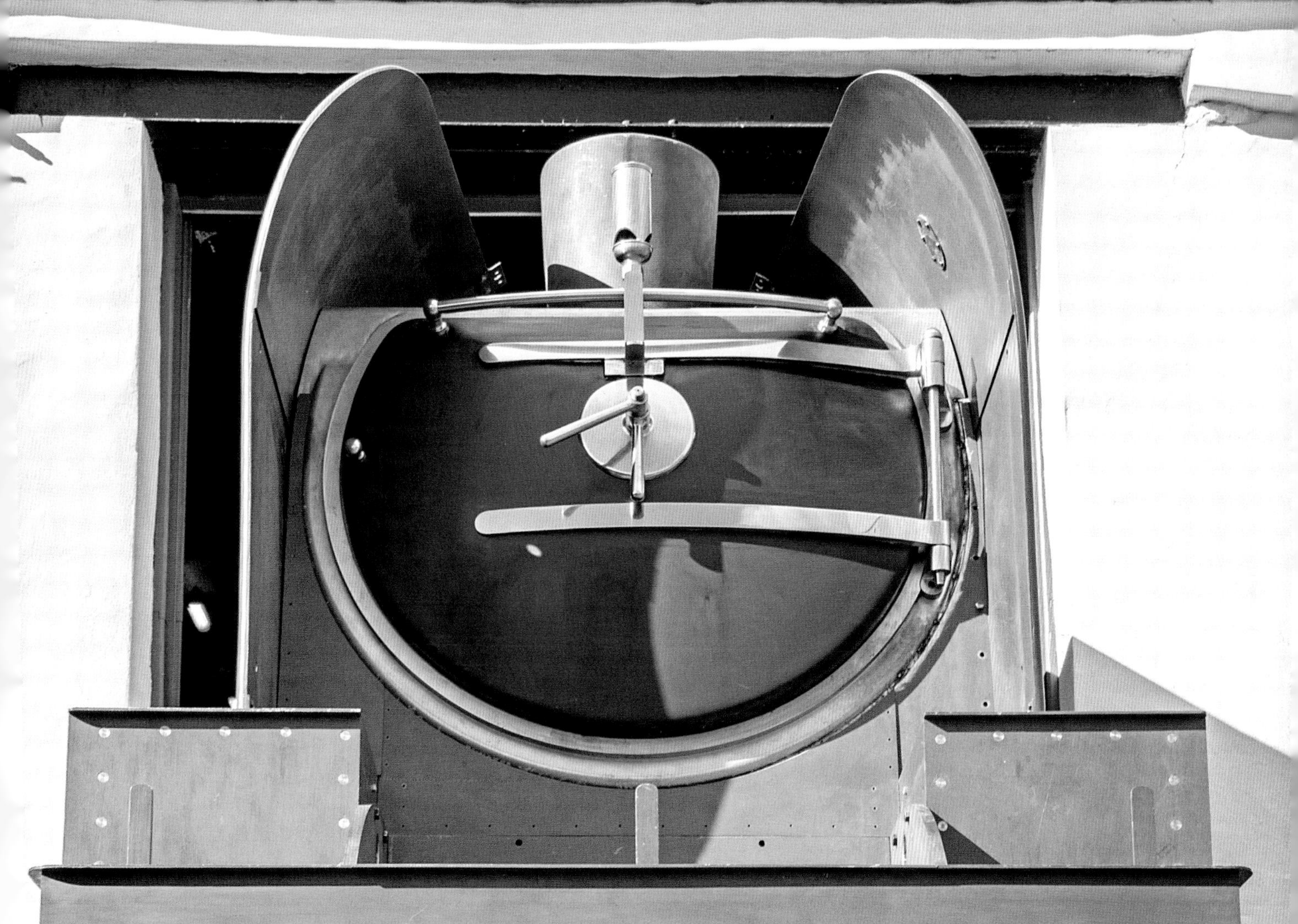

MANDY GRANT

Chapter 7

Next in LINE

Not one to rest on its laurels, the A1 Steam Trust is already preparing to build a V4.

Although P2 2007 *Prince of Wales* is still some way off being completed, the A1 Steam Locomotive Trust is already gearing up to construct its third locomotive. This time it has chosen to build a Gresley V4, which will carry the number 3403, with a name to be decided at a later date. Only two examples were built by the LNER – 3401 *Bantam Cock* and 3402, which was unofficially known as Bantam Hen – both being constructed at Doncaster works. The name of *Bantam Cock* derived from the lightweight nature of the class. Both were cut up at Doncaster Works in 1957.

The V4s represented the last locomotives to be designed by Sir Nigel Gresley, having been designed in the late 1930s, with an envisaged building date of 1939. The outbreak of the Second World War saw this delayed until 1941.

The objective of creating the V4s was to build a locomotive that had the capability to work over routes that were barred to the successful V2s, due to route availability issues. With a RA of 4, the V4s were able to work over about 80% of the LNER network, particularly in East Anglia and Scotland. Gresley's death in 1941, just six weeks after 3401 had emerged from Doncaster Works, coupled with the outbreak of war curtailed what would have been further orders for the class. Indeed, an order for 10 more, for which cylinders had already been cast, was cancelled by Edward Thompson, Gresley's successor.

Gresley employed numerous design methods to keep the weight of the locomotives down, using alloy steels, integrally forged pistons and rods, and three, small 15in cylinders supplied by a high-pressure (250psi) boiler to produce tractive effort. Spurred on by the success of the Gresley V2s, the V4s had many features in common with the class, including a monobloc casting for the cylinders and the same pony truck design. The boiler design incorporated 2% nickel steel plate to reduce its thickness and tapered from 5ft 4in at the firebox to 4ft 8in at the smokebox; the wide firebox allowed the burning of lower quality fuel. No. 3402 was fitted with a welded steel firebox with thermic syphons. This, however, proved to be troublesome, leading to it being replaced with a copper firebox in 1945.

Following a number of trials in the Leeds/York area and in East Anglia, both locomotives were transferred to Scotland where they worked passenger services in and around Edinburgh before moving to the Glasgow-Fort William line in 1943. They performed best on the faster stretches of this line, but the K4s were more sure-footed on the steeper gradients.

Replaced by B1 4-6-0s and Stanier 4-6-0 Black Fives in 1949, the two locomotives moved to Eastfield, and operated goods trains to Edinburgh, Perth and Kinross. Occasionally they worked passenger services in the 1950s, and for a while No. 61700 (LNER No. 3401) was based at Stirling shed specifically for passenger services.

In 1954 they were both transferred to Aberdeen to replace O7 WD 'Austerity' locomotives which were deemed unsuitable for the required fast running. This was to be their last shed before withdrawal three years later.

History has judged the V4s to be the right engines at the wrong time. Had war not broken out and Gresley lived long enough to develop the design, a class of useful 'go anywhere' mixed traffic locomotives would have been extremely useful in the north and east of the LNER's territory. As it was, Thompson decided to opt for the robust simplicity of the B1 design, sacrificing elegance of design and useful route availability in the process for ruggedness and ease of maintenance, which, in light of the operating strictures of the war and the subsequent nationalisation, was probably the pragmatic choice.

An air pump for the 3403.
DAVID ELLIOTT

THE NEW BUILD

To date the A1 Trust has accumulated a number of components to enable the construction of the V4 to fully get under way once 2007 *Prince of Wales* is complete. These include a complete set of fully certified tyres for the new Gresley class V4's pony, Cartazzi and 5ft 8in driving wheels.

They have been purchased from David Buck, owner of Thompson class B1 4-6-0 No. 61306 *Mayflower*, along with a chimney, two BR class 08 shunter speedometer drive generators and two two-stage single spindle air pumps of Finnish origin, including lubricator pumps and check valves for use on No. 2007.

Originally the tyres had been manufactured in South Africa during the late 1990s, for Doncaster scrap merchant Malcolm Barlow, who launched the now defunct Gresley V4 Society in 1994, with a view to building a member of the class. The parts, including a number of B1 components, were salvaged by Malcolm Barlow from Doncaster Works as part of a job lot, which were subsequently acquired by the A1 Trust, who also sourced more than 500 original Gresley

Tyres for the 3403. DAVID ELLIOTT

Class V4 drawings from Malcolm. Significant progress has been made in reviewing and cataloguing these drawings in advance of their scanning into the trust's CAD system.

The V4 construction will also see a further partnership with The Gresley Society Trust which funded the smokebox for No. 2007 *Prince of Wales* as part of the fulfilment of legacy request. The two organisations will work together to manufacture the shared 5ft 8in driving wheel pattern for the new Gresley class V4 No. 3403 and the Gresley Society's Great Northern Railway Gresley class N2 No. 1744.

The class N2, which celebrates its centenary in 2021, is currently under overhaul and requires two replacement driving wheels. The production of the pattern will be project-managed by the A1 Trust and funded by the Gresley Society Trust, with its first use being for No. 1744.

Trustee and P2 project director Mark Allatt said: "We are in the pre-launch phase of the project to build our third new main line steam locomotive, with the detailed review and cataloguing of over 500 acquired drawings, the production of the fundraising strategy and the decision on the high-level specification of No. 3403.

"We want to be ready to start assembling our new Gresley class V4 as soon as our new class P2 is completed. We anticipate the project costing around £3m and taking around five years subject to the pace of fundraising. Our new Gresley class V4 is an ideal locomotive for regional main line tours, repeat main line itineraries and the longer, main line connected heritage railways.

"Unlike with our class P2, where we have had to do a considerable amount of development work to complete the job that Sir Nigel Gresley started in 1934, there will be very little redesign work needed as there were no known problems with the Gresley class V4s.

"In addition, we are delighted to be working with The Gresley Society Trust to produce the 5ft 8in driving wheel pattern shared by the class V4s and N2s.

"Although there is no specific appeal open for No. 3403 yet, any donations made towards it will be ring-fenced for the project.

"The next steps will be to launch a website for the project and The Founders Club to fund the early stages of the project. More announcements will be made during 2019 as the project builds up steam."

THE A1 STEAM LOCOMOTIVE TRUST HAS DECIDED ON:

A P2-style electrical system which is in itself developed from that successfully implemented on the A1

Air plus vacuum brakes as on both A1 and P2 but with only one air pump due to the limited space available

An all-steel, all-welded boiler with no thermic syphon – the one originally fitted to No. 3402 provided no discernible benefit and was removed in 1945

A tender based on the LNER 4200-gallon – as opposed to 3500-gallon – tender with as much water capacity as possible – modifications made to the A1 and P2 tenders added around 1200 gallons

Roller bearings throughout as with A1 and P2

The new P2 design of crank axle and pony truck

Its monobloc cylinder block casting redesigned as a fabrication as with the P2

As much detailed commonality as possible with A1/P2

Chapter 8

The Darlington Brick Train. DARLINGTON BOROUGH COUNCIL

More New BUILDS

Despite all the attention being given to *Tornado* and the *Prince of Wales*, it's important not to forget other new build projects in the North East.

With all the action around Darlington's standard gauge new builds, we should not forget that North Bay Engineering, based in the town, has also built two narrow gauge steam locomotives in recent years. The first of these was a 20-inch steam loco named *Georgina* which entered service at the North Bay Railway in Scarborough in 2016, the firm being the engineering arm of the railway. The latest locomotive to emerge from its works is a blue-liveried Bagnall Sipat-type 0-4-0, named *Otter*, which has gone to the Isle of Man's Groudle Glen Railway. In recent years Groudle Glen Railway volunteers have been working with North Bay Engineering, helping with patterns and designs related to the Sipats. The engineering firm is now concentrating all its efforts on building replica Southwold Railway 2-4-0 *Blyth*, with a view to it entering service in late 2020.

This is a new version of the 3ft gauge Sharp Stewart 2850, which dated from 1879 and was scrapped along with the other locomotives that operated on the railway in 1941 after spending 12 years in open storage following the closure of the line.

Costing £300,000, the project has been broken down into seven stages, the first of these being the construction of the boiler. The Two-Four-0 Club, created by the Southwold Railway Trust, is sponsoring many parts for the locomotive and is expected, thanks to help from a recent legacy, to have funded about half of the project by the time it is completed. Other components that have been fabricated include the smokebox door and chimney.

Although the long-term objective is to restore at least part of the railway, which was open between 1879 and 1929, the new locomotive will initially be confined to a running line of 80ft, located on a one-acre site near Blythe Road. This 'Steamworks' site is being financed by the operation of a miniature railway around the nature reserve, with the main part of the site being home to an engine shed and station buildings, along with a platform and section of 3ft demonstration line. The next objective, with regards to developing the site, is to extend the running line by half a mile from Southwold station and down to the harbour, running alongside the original track bed.

There is also a 3ft gauge museum under development, which will be used to display 3ft rolling stock, including Peckett 0-6-0 *Scaldwell*, which dates from 1913, and a former mining diesel which dates from 1969.

ANOTHER BUILDING PROJECT

Another, often forgotten, steam loco building project is also taking place near Shildon. Although not as glamorous as an A1 or P2, the Class G5 Locomotive Company's project to create a North Eastern Railway G5 0-4-4 is making steady progress, well away from the limelight.

Launched in 2007 by a small group of enthusiasts, it is envisaged that the Wordsell designed loco will initially be confined to heritage railways, but may well make its debut on the national network at some time in the future.

3171 and 3453 leaving Embsay on October 19, 2018. JOHN HUNT

The autocar at the Embsay and Bolton Abbey Railway, prior to restoration commencing. SIMON GOTT

3170 and 3453 near Bow Bridge on October 19, 2018. JOHN HUNT

Removing the paint from the interior of the autocar. SIMON GOTT

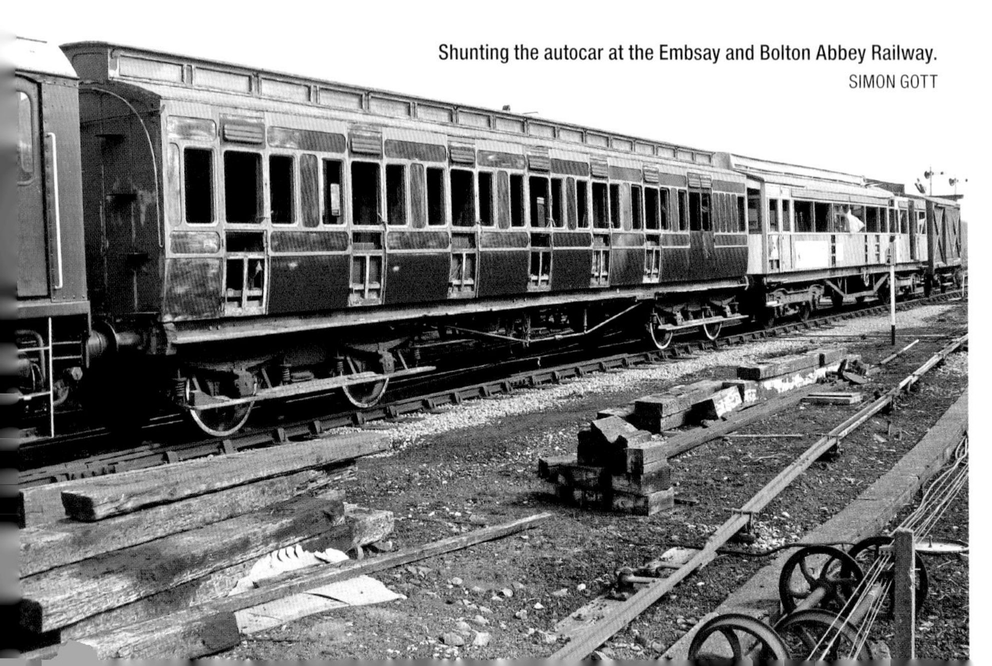
Shunting the autocar at the Embsay and Bolton Abbey Railway. SIMON GOTT

Dating from 1893, the G5s were intended to replace the Class A 2-4-2s, with 110 rolling off the production line at Darlington's North Road Works between 1894 and 1910. The locos were popular branch line performers and 21 examples had push-pull equipment installed.

Away from branch line work, the G5s could be seen operating around Middlesbrough, Leeds and Newcastle. The formation of the LNER allowed members of the class to spread their wings away from the North East and instead they could be seen in action around Aberdeen and Cambridge.

Although withdrawals commenced in the 1940s, the majority of the class made it into the British Rail era. It was the mass introduction of diesel units that, like so many other tank locos up and down Britain, spelt the end for the G5s, with mass inroads being made into their ranks between 1955 and 1958, the final member of the class succumbing in December 1958. As with so many north-eastern steam locos, none escaped the cutting torch.

Following in the footsteps of *Tornado* and *Prince of Wales*, the G5 – which will assume the NER identity 1759 – will have some modifications made to it, compared to the original, due to advances in engineering and the changed certification process. Many of the major components, including the all-welded steel boiler, are now at Shildon, with the main frames having already been completed and the smokebox, cylinder block and drag box having already been installed.

It is hoped that, subject to funding, 1759 will be finished in 2022, with much of the funding being sourced privately. A club has been created to support the project and this has an objective of raising £90,000 to pay for the motion. Supporters can also become shareholders for a minimum payment of £100.

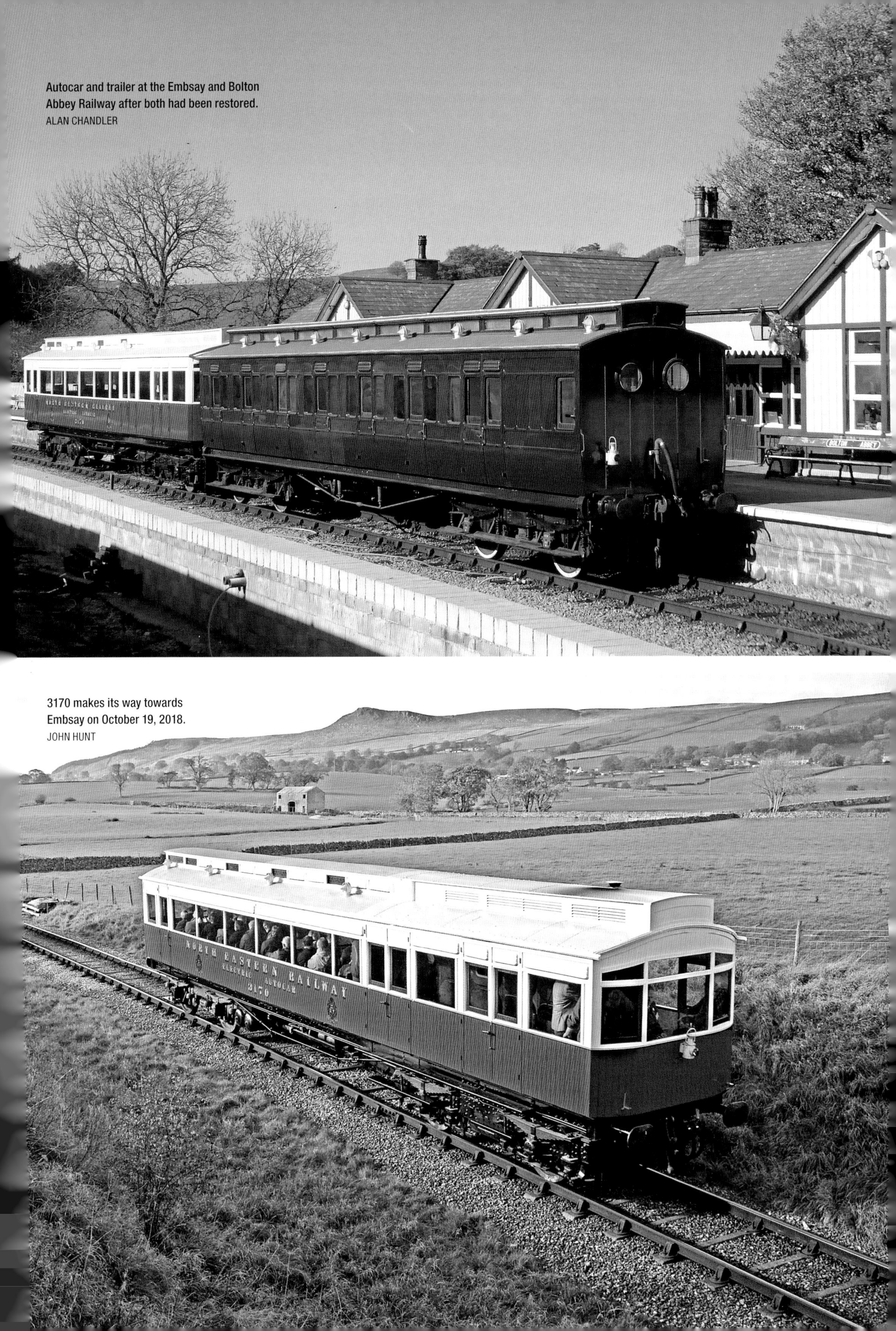

Autocar and trailer at the Embsay and Bolton Abbey Railway after both had been restored.
ALAN CHANDLER

3170 makes its way towards Embsay on October 19, 2018.
JOHN HUNT

Autocar frame undergoes testing at the Great Central Railway on March 17, 2016.
BOTH ALAN CHANDLER

Chapter 9

Lesser known PRESERVATION GROUPS

Looking at the lesser known, but just as important, preservation groups in and around Darlington.

One of the lesser known preservation movements in the town is the Darlington Railway Preservation Society. It was formed during the summer of 1980 following the realisation, after a chance conversation between Barry Cox and Barrie Lamb, that the most important place in the world for railways had no working preserved steam locomotives. After gathering their thoughts and discovering there was support from the North Road Museum Friends Society and the local enthusiast community, it was decided to form a preservation society.

The initial main aim of the newly formed society was to purchase a steam locomotive. At the time 69023 *Joem* was being offered for sale, with a date of the end of 1980 being set by the owner for offers to be made. This short deadline proved too much of a hurdle for the society to raise the necessary funds so, reluctantly, it had to withdraw from its negotiations with the owner. Although it had been in existence in all but name for the previous few months, it was not until January 1981 that the Darlington Railway Preservation Society was formally launched. During the first meeting that month Geoff Jackson said that BR Standard 78018, then based at the Battlefield Line, was for sale. Realising that this could be the last opportunity to purchase a Darlington-built steam locomotive, the society devoted all its efforts in securing it and after a visit to the Battlefield Line to inspect it, an agreement to purchase it was agreed with owner Bill Barton.

This followed a report from the boiler inspector who deemed the boiler to be in good condition. Fundraising then went into overdrive, as did efforts in securing a site from which to work on the locomotive. The society eventually found a home at Henry Boots' yard, where 78018 was dismantled over a period of three years before the components were transferred to its workshop at the North Road Museum. In addition to owning 78018, the society also owns a number of industrial locomotives. The most well-known of these is Peckett 2142 *Northern Gas Board No.1*, dating from 1953 and delivered new to Thompson Street Gas Works, Stockton-on-Tees, and was moved in 1964 to Darlington Gas Works for one year before going to St Anthony's Tar Works in Newcastle. The society purchased 2142 in 1982 after it had been withdrawn in 1978 and dumped on an isolated siding. It arrived at its current location the next year following 12 months' storage at A V Dawson's yard in Middlesbrough. It was initially displayed outside the North Road Museum, with restoration starting in December 1983. The next year 2142 passed its boiler test and entered service. Since then, in addition to operating over the society's short running line, it has gone on hire to Telford Steam Railway and the Cholsey and Wallingford Railway, proving very popular at both lines. The society's collection of diesels consists of Fowler *185-David Payne*, an 0-4-0 diesel mechanical shunter built in 1950 which worked at Cleveland Bridge Engineering; *Derwent 2*, an 0-4-0 Ruston & Hornsby Diesel Electric built in 1949 which worked at Whessoe Engineering Ltd; a Rushton 0-4-0 diesel shunter and a Drury 0-4-0 diesel shunter that was formerly in use at Hartlepool Docks. The society also owns a GEC four-wheel electric locomotive, dating from 1928. The locomotive spent its life at the chemical works on West Auckland Road, Darlington, transferring wagons to the LNER/BR sidings on the Barnard Castle line. Two Wickham trolleys also belong to the society – 965096, dating from 1957, which started its working life based at the Greenfield Works at Gateshead, and MPP0007, dating from 1973.

HISTORICALLY SIGNIFICANT

Formed more than two decades ago, another lesser known preservation group is the Durham Locomotive Preservation Group, which is currently restoring RSH tank loco 77 *Norwood* at the National Railway Museum's Shildon outpost, where working parties are held most weekends. *Norwood* is historically significant as it was the last working industrial steam locomotive, outside of preservation, in the North East. Although fundraising over the last few years has enabled a number of components to be purchased, fundraising is an ongoing concern, which has been boosted thanks to a small grant from the Banks Foundation. The group is also exploring other avenues from which grant funding can be obtained. *Norwood* was ordered from Robert Stephenson & Hawthorn

FOCAL POINT

Although not involved in locomotive restoration, the North Eastern Railway Association was formed in 1961 as a focal point for interest in the North Eastern Railway, its predecessors, its contemporaries and its successors.

After more than half a century of active research, recording and curation, the NERA now possesses an archival resource that reflects the company, along with the industrial, social and commercial history of the North East of England and its people.

NERA members' interests cover all aspects of operations of the railway – from locomotives, rolling stock, stations and signalling, through to timetabling, shipping and road vehicles – offering a broad base of experience and insight for the general enthusiast, the model maker, the researcher or those that are just curious. The NERA also has an active programme of meetings held throughout the year at venues in York, Darlington, Hull and London. There is also a supporting programme of seminars, visits, walks and tours.

The driver and fireman of 78018 wait to depart Ramsbottom on March 12, 2019. GORDON EDGAR

Ltd by Priestman Collieries on January 22, 1947, order number N61. In August 1948 it was a prime exhibit at Manors station, as part of the Stephenson centenary exhibition. In addition to *Norwood* the Durham Locomotive Preservation Group also owns LMS brake van 730202. Initially this was on loan to the group from the Bowes Railway, but in 2005 an agreement was reached where the locomotive group purchased it. During its LMS and BR service, 730202 was based mainly at Ashington and Lynemouth, before being purchased by the Bowes railway, where its long wheelbase made it unsuitable for negotiating Springwell yard. One of 670 such vehicles built to lot 919, 730202 emerged from Derby in 1938 and originally had no vacuum brakes, relying only on a hand brake. The Durham Locomotive Preservation Group has now fully restored the brake van and it is hired out to Locomotion, at Shildon, to enable the National Railway Museum to offer brake van rides around its site.

69023 is seen shortly after entering preservation. ARMSTRONG RAILWAY PHOTOGRAPHIC TRUST

Chapter 10

Weardale RAILWAY

A popular heritage railway with ambitious plans for the future.

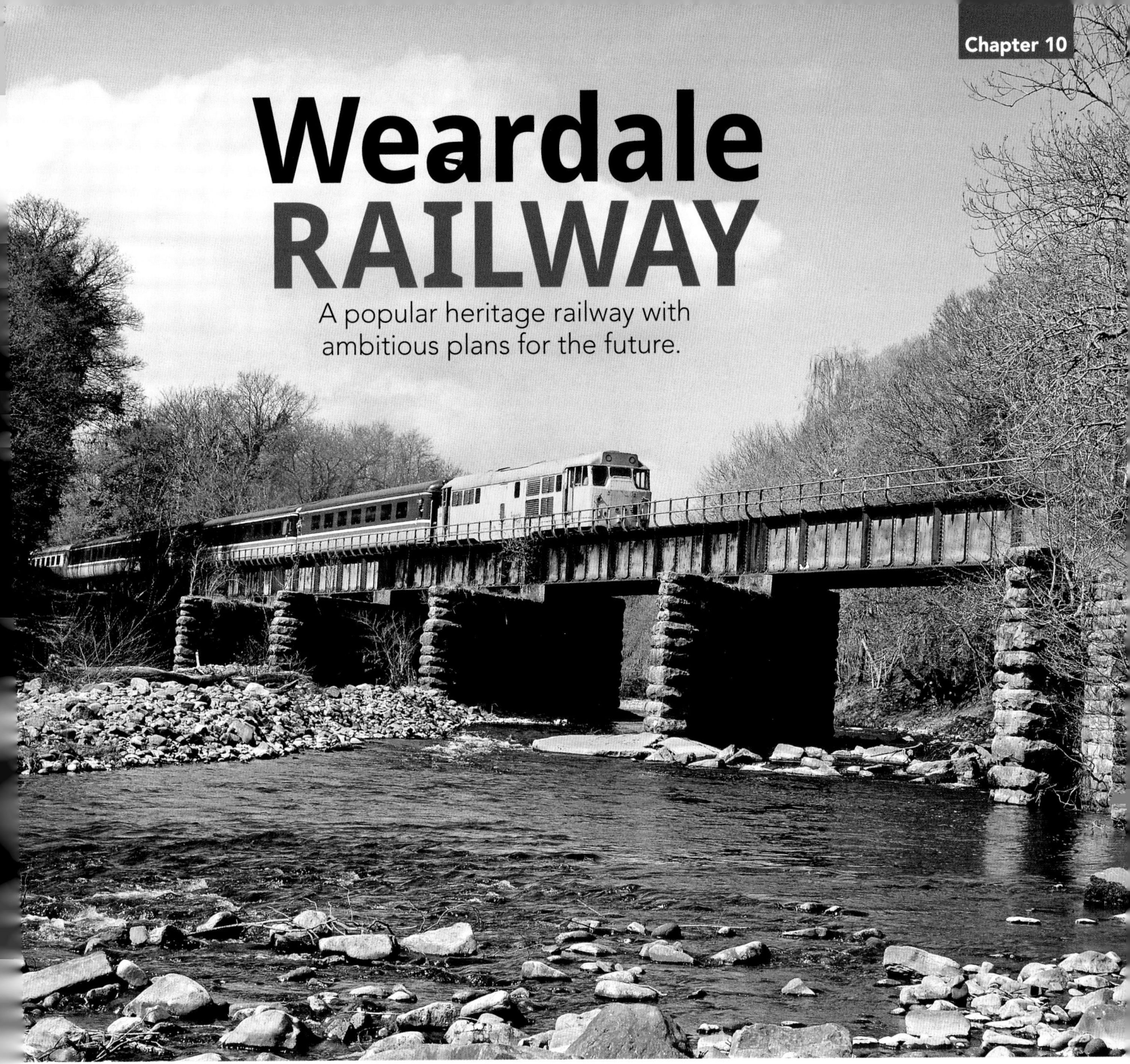

31285 crossing Wolsingham Bridge on April 21, 2018. JOHN ASKWITH

The final extension of the Weardale Railway to Wearhead opened on October 21, 1895. Between Eastgate and Westgate at Cambo Keels, sidings were established to serve the Weardale Iron Company's Heights limestone quarry, which is still in operation today.

The Wearhead branch lost its passenger trains in 1953, although the main closures came in the 1960s, post the Beeching Axe. Services to Barnard Castle via West Auckland finished in 1962, with those to Durham being abolished two years later, and services to Crook in 1965. These closures left only the former original Stockton and Darlington line to Darlington line in use, along with the freight-only branch serving Eastgate.

Recognising the potental of the route, Durham County Council supported the introduction of leisure services and, under the patronage of David Bellamy, intermittent specials began to operate to Stanhope again in 1983 under the banner of 'The Heritage Line', a nod to the route's association with the Stockton and Darlington Railway. This became a scheduled British Rail weekend-only summer service, which even made it into the national timetable, between May 23, 1988 and September 27, 1992, with Etherley, otherwise known as Witton Park Station, reopening on August 21, 1991.

In March 1993, due to rising costs, Lafarge took the decision to service the Eastgate cement works by road, thus ending its reliance on rail. In turn, British Rail then announced its intention to close the line due to the loss of revenue from this traffic. Local authorities wasted no time in trying to seek out another use for the line and after careful consideration, concluded that the only immediate possibility was a steam-hauled heritage railway.

The Weardale Railway preservation project was launched in 1993, with the initial ambition to start running a steam service along the scenic western section. The operating company was known as Weardale Railways Ltd, a company limited by guarantee.

PROMINENT ROLE

The Weardale Railway Trust is a voluntary group whose members are supporters of the project. It was initially envisaged that the Weardale Railway Trust would just be a 'supporters' club' but it assumed a more prominent role due to Weardale Railways Ltd getting into difficulties. This resulted in the Weardale Railway Trust taking a 12.5% minority stake in the ownership of Weardale Railways Ltd in 2006.

By now things were on a roll and confidence in the project saw large amounts of public sector grant finance

Single car DMU 55012 crosses Etherley Viaduct with a service for Bishop Auckland on July 14, 2018.
JOHN ASKWITH

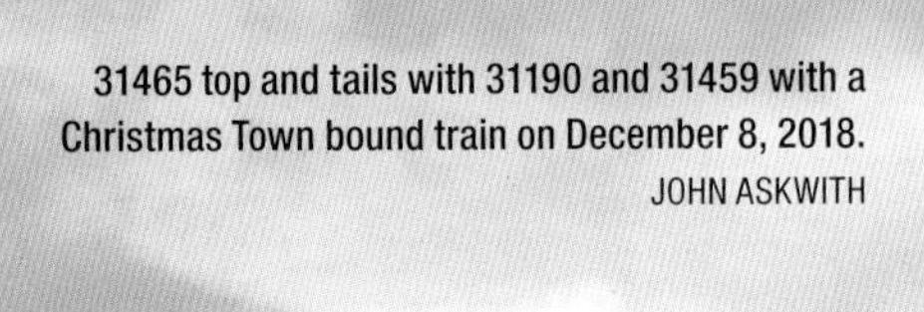

31465 top and tails with 31190 and 31459 with a Christmas Town bound train on December 8, 2018. JOHN ASKWITH

obtained or conditionally pledged from various donors, including the Regional Development Agency (One NorthEast), Durham County Council and the Wear Valley District Council. The Manpower Services Commission contributed to the wages of paid staff, a very welcome move in what had become an area of high unemployment, and this allowed a 40-strong workforce to be recruited, a depot and base of operations to be established at Wolsingham and the station at Stanhope to be restored. Passenger services commenced in July 2004, initially running from Wolsingham to Stanhope but with the eventual aspiration of extending them along the full length of the remaining line. There were even plans to rebuild the Eastgate to Wearhead section, which by then had been lifted.

After a while, a community interest company known as Ealing Community Transport agreed to pay £100,000 in return for a 75% stake in Weardale Railways Ltd and to also provide management support to the project. In addition Ealing Community Transport agreed to underwrite any further operating losses incurred by Weardale Railways Ltd. This guarantee was sufficient to enable the creditors of Weardale Railways Ltd to permit the resumption of limited services on the line in August 2006.

In September 2008, Ealing Community Transport's 75% stake in WRC was transferred to British American Railway Services, a wholly owned subsidiary of US private company Iowa Pacific Holdings. Ed Ellis, the spokesman for these firms, visited the Weardale Railway in October 2008, and announced the company's ambition to reopen the line to Bishop Auckland by the end of 2008. This announcement galvanised staff and volunters and, in October 2008, they carried out the 'Brush Blitz' to clear 14 years' worth of vegetation growth from the track between Wolsingham and Bishop Auckland. Following repairs to two damaged sections of track during early 2009, a passenger-carrying Wickham trolley was able to journey along the line from Wolsingham to within sight of Bishop Auckland station. Ellis also announced plans to build a rail freight terminal at Eastgate for the loading of aggregates from local quarries together with other freight, including mineral, food and agricultural traffic.

RECONNECTION

On March 27, 2009 the company announced that Network Rail had agreed to reinstall missing points and crossings at Bishop Auckland to reconnect the Weardale Line with the national rail network.

It was stated that this would be carried out before July 31, 2009.

Network Rail completed the connection in early September 2009. On September 29, 2009, the development of the Eastgate Renewable Energy Village received unanimous outline approval by the County Durham strategic planning committee, this being perceived as a potential giant boost to the line's future prospects. However, by 2013 this project had gone very quiet.

In December 2009, UK Coal indicated that it was interested in using the line to transport coal from an opencast coal mine and that local quarry owners had been approached about the possibility of transporting aggregates over the route.

Her Majesty's Railway Inspectorate travelled along the Weardale line inspecting bridges, fences and crossings on January 25, 2010. Luckily, it was discovered that only a few minor works were required to make the route fit

Bubble Car E55012 crossing Wolsingham Bridge on September 30, 2017. JOHN ASKWITH

for carrying passengers, these being completed in time for a London King's Cross to Stanhope charter train to run in February 2010; this became the first main line passenger service to travel along the line since the 1980s.

This ground-breaking working was followed on February 27 by another charter service, this time from Crewe to Stanhope, and operated by Spitfire Railtours.

Regular passenger services to Bishop Auckland commenced on May 23, 2010, but for the 2013 operating season a scheduled service was not offered, the railway instead offering themed operations, such as Dine and Ride and the Polar Express. Since 2014, the Railway Trust has operated passenger trains on selected weekdays and weekends mainly using a class 122 DMU. Initially, this only ran between Wolsingham and Stanhope but, on March 27, 2016, this service was extended to Witton-le-Wear. In April 2018, the Weardale Railway CIC announced that works had commenced to lift a short section of track at Broken Banks, just west of Bishop Auckland, to enable the embankment to be repaired after subsidence had made the line unusable for passenger traffic.

Since July 2018, two of the three daily return services between Stanhope and Witton-le-Wear have been extended to Bishop Auckland West station.

COAL TRAIN

After receiving planning permission to load opencast coal, mined in the Crook

area, alterations were carried out to the Weardale Railway's Wolsingham depot, to enable it to receive and transship the coal from road to rail.

The first loaded coal train left Wolsingham on June 16, 2011 bound for Scunthorpe steel works. Later, services were extended to include the power station at Ratcliffe on Soar. This become a five-train-a-week operation until October 2, 2013, and ceased as a result of the financial collapse of UK Coal, following the spoil tip landslip that destroyed the connecting railway at Hatfield Colliery in February 2013, preventing coal shipments, along with an underground fire at Daw Mill Colliery the following month which had a devastating impact on UK Coal, forcing it into a financial crisis.

Chapter 11

Shildon Works

Although long gone, Shildon Works forms an important part of the story.

Famous for being the terminus of the Stockton and Darlington Railway when it opened in 1825, Shildon grew to be a prolific builder of wagons.

Following the creation of the British Rail workshops division, Shildon Works underwent a massive £800,000 refurbishment in 1962, equipping it to build and repair wagons. The most famous wagon type to roll off the Shildon production line was the merry-go-round coal wagon, with just over 11,000 being constructed at Shildon. Despite being built in such large numbers, only a handful made it into preservation, their aluminium bodies being highly prized by scrap metal merchants. Other wagons to be built at Shildon included Presflo cement wagons and Freightliner wagons.

Just 20 years later the announcement that Shildon Works would close was made. The news, which was announced on April 23, 1982, sent shock waves throughout the local community and the rail industry as a whole. Such was the importance of the works to the local economy that it was responsible for the employment of 86% of the male workforce manufacturing jobs in the town. At the time of the announcement 2600 people were employed there.

Rumours had begun circulating about the works closing for more than a week

Hunslet *Austerity* 3890 of 1964 arrives at Chasewater Heath sidings with MGR wagons as '6678' (Hunslet 6678 built in 1969) waits with internal NCB mineral wagons. The 233hp 0-4-0 diesel-hydraulic was supplied new to NCB Maryport Disposal Point, Cumbria. It was moved to Widdrington, Northumberland in 1981, then to Bennerley Disposal Point, Derbyshire in 1982 and finally before purchase for preservation to Wentworth Stores South Yorkshire in 1984. *Austerity*, built just five years before the diesel, was purchased new by the National Coal Board South Yorkshire Area, and put to use at Cadeby Main Colliery, Conisborough, being allocated the fleet running number '66'. Fitted with the company's patent gas producer system, designed to eliminate smoke, it was also equipped with an underfeed mechanical stoker, although this is currently not fitted since purchase and restoration by Brian Clifford at the Buckinghamshire Railway Centre.
GORDON EDGAR

EWS 60079 *Foinaven* with Mainline decals heading northbound MGR empties for the Ayrshire coalfield on the early morning of September 4, 1999. GORDON EDGAR

prior to the official announcement, with union officials and British Rail managers deep in negotiation during this period. Such was the secrecy surrounding the talks that journalists had the telephone hung up on them when they tried to speak to union officials at the works. Days before the official announcement, there was a protest outside British Rail's London headquarters.

There followed a trade union march on April 29, which saw more than 5000 people, including children and pensioners, form a procession through the railway town.

British Rail justified the closure by saying: "Shildon is BREL principal wagon-building works and has a capacity to build some 1200-1500 wagons per year, and to repair in excess of 20,000 wagons per year. There are no new build orders in for 1983 and prospects for 1984 and 1985 indicate that future needs are insignificant in relation to the capacity available. Operating Shildon on the substantially reduced repairs workload only would not be viable and would lead to substantial losses in 1983, with no prospect of a return to profit in the future."

May 5 saw a report by Durham and Sedgefield councils, stating that the closure of Shildon Works would result in the loss of 2180 jobs, equating to one in four people covered by the Bishop Auckland Employment Exchange being unemployed. In addition, 450 more people, working for suppliers to the works, would lose their jobs.

At a meeting two days later a number of options were discussed. One of these was a national strike for all BR engineering works. Derby works was reported as being lukewarm to the idea, but Glasgow was much more enthusiastic, believing that Shildon's closure could be the thin end of the wedge with regards to a severe reduction in the number of workshops.

It was decided to charter a train and hold a protest in London, as this was thought to be more effective. Those going to the capital had to pay £5 towards the fare, with the balance being paid for from the fighting fund.

Both Derby and Glasgow went on to suffer a similar fate.

Chapter 12

Newly constructed ScotRail class 385s lined up outside the Newton Aycliffe plant. HITACHI

Plans for 2025

Darlington is preparing for an exciting 2025. We look at what can be expected.

Big plans are afoot to conserve as much as possible of the former Stockton & Darlington route in time for the bicentennial celebrations in 2025. A partnership has been created between the three local authorities, the Tees Valley Combined Authority, the National Railway Museum, Historic England, Friends of the Stockton & Darlington Railway, along with rail industry big players such as Hitachi, whose rolling stock assembly plant sits next to the route, and Network Rail.

Train operators LNER and Northern Rail have also become involved in drawing up exciting and ambitious plans for the event.

A survey has been carried out to determine how much of the original line survives, along with an objective of discovering what needs conserving and how to improve access to the surviving sections of line.

The full route was designated a Heritage Action Zone by Historic England in 2018, opening up the potential for promotion and other resources to make the celebrations a reality.

A proposal to develop the section between Witton Park and Stockton-on-Tees as a cycle route is also under way. There is also an exciting proposal to reintroduce live steam on the route once again and a determined effort is being made to generate a community feeling towards the line, which will help in its long-term survival and conservation. Celebrations to mark the anniversary of the line's opening have been held every 50 years, the last one being in 1975.

Seventeen of the 26 miles of original railway are still operational, with Darlington's Head of Steam museum, the National Railway Museum's outreach facility at Shildon and the Preston Park Museum assisting in telling the story of the world's first passenger railway, but much of the remaining nine miles of route is in a terrible state and is difficult to access.

The S&DR route passes through the territories of the Stockton, Darlington and Durham local authorities.

As anyone who has ever had any professional dealings with councils will tell you, liaising with three such organisations where a place of interest crosses over into a neighbouring council's control can be a nightmare in red tape.

Although each of the three were aware of the importance of the line, it needed a singular point of contact to help coordinate any efforts to raise awareness and deal with any conservation issues. The Friends of the Stockton & Darlington Railway was formed in 2013, solely with this aim.